A Guide to Observation, Participation, and Reflection in the Classroom

FOURTH EDITION

A Guide to Observation, Participation, and Reflection in the Classroom

FOURTH EDITION

Arthea J. S. Reed
University of North Carolina at Asheville

Verna E. Bergemann
University of North Carolina at Asheville

Boston   Burr Ridge, IL   Dubuque, IA   Madison, WI   New York   San Francisco   St. Louis
Bangkok   Bogotá   Caracas   Lisbon   London   Madrid
Mexico City   Milan   New Delhi   Seoul   Singapore   Sydney   Taipei   Toronto

McGraw-Hill Higher Education

A Division of The McGraw-Hill Companies

A GUIDE TO OBSERVATION, PARTICIPATION, AND REFLECTION
IN THE CLASSROOM, FOURTH EDITION

Published by McGraw-Hill, an imprint of The McGraw-Hill Companies, Inc., 1221 Avenue of the Americas, New York, NY 10020. Copyright © 2001, 1998, 1995, 1992 by The McGraw-Hill Companies, Inc. All rights reserved. No part of this publication may be reproduced or distributed in any form or by any means, or stored in a database or retrieval system, without the prior written consent of The McGraw-Hill Companies, Inc., including, but not limited to, in any network or other electronic storage or transmission, or broadcast for distance learning.

This book is printed on recycled, acid-free paper containing 10% postconsumer waste.

1 2 3 4 5 6 7 8 9 0 QPD/QPD 0 9 8 7 6 5 4 3 2 1 0

ISBN 0–07–240106–0

Vice president and editor-in-chief: *Thalia Dorwick*
Editorial director: *Jane E. Vaicunas*
Sponsoring editor: *Beth Kaufman*
Developmental editor: *Teresa Wise*
Marketing manager: *Daniel M. Loch*
Project manager: *Rose Koos*
Production supervisor: *Sandy Ludovissy*
Coordinator of freelance design: *David W. Hash*
Freelance interior designer: *Todd Sanders*
Cover designer: *Nathan Bahls*
Cover image: *©Corbis*
Compositor: *Shepherd, Inc.*
Typeface: *10.5/12 Goudy*
Printer: *Quebecor Printing Book Group/Dubuque, IA*

www.mhhe.com

Brief Contents

Contents

Acknowledgments

Without the help and support of many individuals, this guide would never have been completed.

First and foremost, each of us wishes to thank the other for her contribution to all four editions of this book. Each recognizes not only the professional contribution of the other, but the friendship that has made a 20-year collaboration joyful and valuable. We have been each other's collaborator, colleague, co-author, confidant, mentor, and best friend. Neither of us could have achieved what we have without the other.

Next, we could not have written this book without the help of thousands of students from scores of classrooms during our more than 75 years of cumulative teaching. These students have provided us with laughter, tears, anecdotes, and hopefully, wisdom. We learned from them, and they taught us most of what we know about teaching and learning.

Thanks, too, to our teaching colleagues—those professionals we observed, taught side by side with, shared experiences and ideas with, and learned to love—we appreciate the qualities of their teaching and humanity. Although they are too numerous to mention, we must name a few. Special thanks go to our UNC - A colleagues Sandra Byrd and James E. McGlinn who contributed to this and previous editions. Also, great appreciation goes to Mary W. Olson who helped us author the third edition of this work and has contributed to this edition. Also, thanks to our many good friends and research colleagues at UNC - A's Ramsey Library. Without the technical help of Elizabeth E. Hunt who formatted many of the guide's forms, this book would have never been completed. Also, we cannot forget Don Reed, the best mentor we know, who kept us humble, but allowed us to believe in ourselves and each other.

We also want to thank the reviewers of this edition, David B. Gustavson, Louisana State University, Shreveport; and Nathalie Popham, Wilmington College, Delaware, whose comments helped us make additions in accord with current research, trends, and practice.

Finally, thanks to all of those who have made this edition and the previous editions a reality. Marcuss Oslander, the original editor of this book, has our deepest gratitude. Also, thanks to Beth Kaufman, Education Editor; Terri Wise, Developmental Editor; Rose Koos, Project Manager; Dorothy Wendel, Copy Editor; and Shepherd, Inc., Compositor for their patient, support, and helpful edits.

It goes without saying that without you, the professors who have chosen to utilize this book to help your students become better teachers, the book would not have an audience. Thanks to you and your students for bringing this work to life.

Arthea J. S. (Charlie) Reed
Verna E. Bergemann
Asheville, N.C.

About the Authors

Arthea J. S. Reed, called "Charlie" by her students, family, and friends, lives in Asheville, North Carolina. She taught at the University of North Carolina at Asheville for seventeen years, served as professor and chair of the Education Department, and then became Professor Emeritus at the liberal arts public university. Currently she is Director of Education and Development at Northwestern Mutual Life in Asheville. She received her Ph.D. from Florida State University, her M.S. from Southern Connecticut State University, and her B.S. from Bethany College in West Virginia. She has taught in grades two through twelve in the public schools of Connecticut, Ohio, and West Virginia. She is author of *Reaching Adolescents: The Young Adult Book and the School* (Merrill, 1993), *Comics to Classics: A Guide to Books for Teens and Preteens* (Penguin, 1994), *Presenting Harry Mazer* (Twayne, 1996), and numerous monographs, book chapters, and articles. For six years, she was editor of *The ALAN Review,* a highly regarded journal in the field of young-adult literature. She has been co-editor of the Penguin/Signet Classic teachers guide series since 1988, editing or writing guides to more than thirty classic books and CD-ROMs. She was the chair of the National Council of Teachers of English Promising Young Writers program from 1990–1995 and was of the co-director Mountain Area Writing Project, a site of the national Writing Project, for eight years. In 1996 she served as president of ALAN. She has served on numerous local, state, and national education committees, and in 1985 she was named the Ruth and Leon Feldman Professor by the UNC–A faculty for her service to education. In 2000 she wrote *Norma Fox Mazer: A Writer's World* (Scarecrow).

Verna E. Bergemann is Professor Emeritus and past chair of the Education Department at the University of North Carolina at Asheville, where she taught for twelve years. She currently lives in Marion, North Carolina. Prior to coming to UN1, she was a professor of education at the State University of New York at Oswego for thirteen years. She earned her Ed.D. at the University of Maryland, her M.A. at the State University of New York at Buffalo, and her B.A. at the State University of New York at Brockport. She taught elementary school in Niagara Falls, New York, and Los Alamos, New Mexico. She has worked with beginning teachers as a helping teacher, as a cooperating teacher in a university laboratory school, and as a consultant with the North Carolina Department of Public Instruction. She has been a professor of education at two universities and is the author of numerous articles and activity workbooks for teachers. For many years she has worked closely with volunteer organizations that attempt to improve adult literacy. In 1989, she was named Woman of Distinction and Woman of the Year by the city of Asheville for her outstanding contributions to literacy education. In 1992, she chaired a school-study committee for private schools in Asheville. In 1997, she was selected to appear in the 1997/1998 *Who's Who in the South and Southeast.* In 2000/2001, she continues her work in teacher education, supervising student teachers.

Introduction

A Guide to Observation, Participation, and Reflection in the Classroom, Fourth Edition is written for you, the student. However, it is designed to help you move beyond being a student. It provides you with sequenced school-based observation, teaching experiences, and reflection that not only will bridge the gap between the world of the student and the world of the teacher, but also help you connect the world of theory to the world of practice. In beginning the process of becoming an effective teacher, you must learn to view students, schools, and teachers as a teacher would. In addition, you must develop, practice, and reflect on the skills and techniques of effective teaching in order to perfect them.

The *Guide* is divided into six parts: Part I—Understanding Fieldwork, Part II—Observing in the Schools, Part III—Developing Successful Teaching Skills, Part IV—The Portfolio, Part V—Glossary, and Part VI—Forms. This edition includes expanded approaches to observation and participation, including the reflective process, standards of measuring teaching excellence, teaching to multiple intelligences, identifying teaching styles, and keeping portfolios.

Observation to gain knowledge and understanding must come first. Thus, Chapter 1 presents the importance of early fieldwork, based on the authors' experiences in elementary, secondary, and university classrooms and documented by recent research of teacher educators and by professional organizations that focus on teacher education. The next three chapters of the guide provide examples and methods of anecdotal, structured, and reflective observations of teachers, as well as of classrooms, and students. The observation techniques have been designed to help you become a critical and objective observer.

Once you have had the opportunity to reflect on your observations, Chapters 5 and 6 provide you with guidance for developing a gradual and reflective approach to becoming a teacher and include many of the tools and techniques used by effective teachers. The first part of this section explains the importance of classroom participation during teacher training. The rest of Chapters 5 and 6 provide you with information for preteaching, planning, tutoring, teaching small groups, teaching large groups, and reflecting on your teaching. Chapter 7 will provide you with steps in keeping a portfolio of your preservice experiences in the classroom.

Finally, following the chapters, you will find copies of all the observation and participation forms and instruments that have been discussed throughout this guide, numbered to coincide with the completed samples. These can be removed from the book and duplicated for your use. Each has been extensively field-tested by college and university students over a period of two decades.

The authors of this guide hope that as you complete and reflect on each observation, participation, and teaching activity, you will strengthen your resolve to become an effective teacher.

Arthea J. S. Reed
Verna E. Bergemann
Asheville, NC

A Guide to Observation, Participation, and Reflection in the Classroom

FOURTH EDITION

PART I

Understanding Fieldwork

Chapter One
The Importance of Fieldwork

The 1999 report, "Teacher Quality: A Report on the Preparation and Qualification of Public School Teachers" (U.S. Department of Education), concluded that preservice teachers do not spend enough time in elementary and secondary schools during their preservice training. The report emphasized that early field experiences play an important role in shaping and maintaining high-quality teachers. When Dalphia Raye Pierce, teacher educator at Utah State University, asked secondary teachers about the kinds of training experiences they had in teacher preparation, the most frequent complaint they voiced was they were not given the opportunity to work with students until reaching student-teaching status or on-the-job-training. The teachers thought that was too late and that they needed earlier field experiences during their first courses in their teacher-preparation program (Pierce 1996, 223). However, a 1997 survey sponsored by the American Association of Colleges for Teacher Education (AACTE) revealed that teacher-preparation candidates receive substantial early field experiences. According to the survey, 79 percent of elementary-education teacher-preparation programs and 49 percent of secondary programs require students to spend more than 90 hours in classrooms prior to student teaching. The colleges and universities that participated in this survey, which was conducted by three Southwest Texas State University teacher educators, concur that field experiences for teacher-preparation candidates must be increasingly complex. Early field experiences involved preservice teachers shadowing elementary and secondary students, engaging in general classroom observation, participating in focused observations, then gradually assisting teachers in directed tasks such as bulletin board preparation, grading students' papers, working with small groups of students, and eventually teaching the entire class. In addition, preservice teachers in these institutions were taught to observe the contextual features of the classroom, school, and community. It appears from these studies that new teachers believe that they needed more time observing and participating in the classrooms in which they were being trained to teach, while the colleges and universities they attended can document significant fieldwork in their training programs. Why the dichotomy?

The need for more preservice time spent in real classrooms is acknowledged by teacher-education institutions as well as by beginning teachers. However, increasing the time spent off campus in public school settings is frequently impractical. So, what is the answer? There could be more than one, including increasing the length of teacher-education training programs. However, again, this may be impractical. Hence, the best answer seems to lie in improving the quality rather than the quantity of preservice teacher observation and participation.

The National Council for Accreditation of Teacher Education (NCATE), a national accrediting agency of teacher-education programs, sets aside clinical and field-based experiences as one of its major standards for accreditation of teacher-education programs. The NCATE also suggests that it is not only the quantity of experiences that is important, but that the experiences must be systematic and provide opportunities for preservice teachers to observe, plan, and practice their skills in a variety of settings and with culturally diverse and exceptional populations (NCATE 1997, 20). These field experiences should encourage

reflection by the preservice teacher, as well as feedback from university and public-school faculty and the student's peers. According to the National Association of State Education Chiefs (NASTEC), 38 states now require a specified number of field-experience hours prior to student teaching, from a low of 40 clock hours in Washington to a high of 300 in Ohio (NASTEC 1999). Likewise, the importance of field experiences has been recognized by the Educational Testing Service (ETS) in the redesign of its national examination used in many states prior to teacher licensure or certification. The series of tests, previously called the *National Teachers Examination*, is now called *Praxis*, acknowledging the role of practice and reflection in teacher training. Included within the series of examinations are tests that require students to apply their academic knowledge in classroom situations. The Association for Childhood Education International (ACEI) states that field experiences for preservice teachers should be carefully sequenced so there will be a gradual increase of responsibility in the classroom. Likewise, the ACEI believes that preservice teachers must be provided with opportunities to work with students who come from culturally diverse backgrounds and possess diverse abilities, including mainstreamed or special-education students (ACEI 1997, 167).

John Goodlad, an education professor and researcher at University of Washington, Seattle, asked senior teacher-education students to rank on a seven-point scale the most beneficial aspects of their programs. Not surprisingly, they ranked in this order: social foundations courses (3.8), educational psychology (4.9), general methods courses (5.2), field experiences prior to student teaching (6.0), and at the top, student teaching (6.7). However, although field experiences are considered to be exceedingly valuable, teacher-education students and faculty tend to agree that the most effective field experiences are well-organized, well-planned, and allow for reflection (1990, 247). Authors H. Frederick Sweitzer and Mary A. King report that field experiences in teacher-education programs afford future teachers the opportunity for:

- Understanding the complexities of teaching.
- Personal growth.
- Self-knowledge.
- Clarifying career and educational goals (1999, 4).

A study conducted at Alverno College affirms these contentions. Preservice teachers who had extensive structured and developmentally sequenced field experiences in a variety of settings prior to student teaching graduated with more conviction and confidence about teaching. According to this study, 93.5 percent of those students in the experimental group were self-assured and confident about their knowledge of teaching skills and subject area as compared to 33.6 percent of the students who graduated in teacher education without the extensive field experiences (U.S. Department of Eduation 1999, 4).

In a study of elementary teacher-education seniors at the University of Central Arkansas, Carol Anne Pierson asked the students to reflect on the field experiences they had prior to student teaching. They identified four priorities to ensure successful experiences:

- Clear expectations and objectives for the field experiences; knowing what to look for so as not to miss significant events in initial observations.
- Opportunity for feedback and discussion about the experience to help students understand what they were learning.
- Careful correlation of the field experience with the theory and/or method taught in the college classroom.
- Well-defined procedures for the field experiences (1993, 288).

This chapter and those following are designed to help you get the most from your preservice, practical field experiences. This chapter provides you with guidelines for a gradual, reflective approach to beginning teaching. Chapters 2, 3, and 4 provide you with techniques for observing teachers, students, classrooms, schools, and curriculum. Chapters 5 and 6 give you tools to plan your teaching, organize what and how you will teach, and reflect upon your experience. Chapter 7 helps you develop a portfolio of your teaching as you reflect on your field experiences and prepare to teach. Because the practical experiences our students have in the classroom prior to their student teaching are so critical to their development as teachers, we have spent more than two decades developing, adapting, revising, and field-testing these forms. If you use them carefully, we believe they will help you get the most from your preservice teaching experiences.

Careful Observation: Your First Task

Observation is one effective means of learning how certain teaching methods are employed in the schools, how classrooms are organized, and how students respond to the classroom environment. This guide will provide you with information on the processes of observation and participation in general and with specific forms that can be used in specific classroom situations. It is helpful to keep a journal or log of the observations you make, even during field experiences in which you are primarily teaching. Here's an example of one such anecdotal log from a student teacher. You will notice that there is no attempt to record all of the events of the day. This log can then be used as the student teacher reflects on his observations and his teaching with his school-based cooperating teacher and college or university supervisor. It and other log entries like it can become a part of his portfolio.

OBSERVATION AND TEACHING LOG

OBSERVER: Michael Kealohalan Anderson

GRADE: Fourth

JANUARY 3, 20—first day of school

Oh, my goodness, so many unusual names to remember. The students seem to be excited to be back at the school. The schedule of the day is complicated (new to me). Students change classes at certain times during the day. Each teacher has a specialty that he or she teaches. Regardless of the specialty of the individual, each teacher must teach reading, spelling, and their specialty to their homeroom class. For example, my cooperating teacher (Ms. Owenbey) teaches reading, spelling, and computers to her homeroom. Then at 10:25 the students change classes. Then Ms. Owenbey teaches computers the remaining periods of the day.

JANUARY 4, 20—Rain and rain. It's been raining for days now. Today I took the "roll." It is really helping me learn the students' names. After spelling and reading we had health. Oh, what a long day this has been. Health could surely be covered in the science class.

JANUARY 7, 20—Nice weekend, no rain. However it is raining today. Yuk. The children seem to be getting back into the groove of school. Overall, I would say they seem to tolerate it without too much resistance.

JANUARY 8, 20—Ms. Owenbey showed me how the students worked together on their "spelling kit." It is an interesting setup. The students are placed in pairs according to their ability to spell. They then go over lists of words out loud—taking turns, of course. Then, they each give one another a test by calling the words out while the other writes them down. This list is then checked by having the student call back the words they have spelled and checking for mistakes. The misspelled words are put on a separate piece of paper for further study. The students switch roles and go through the process again. After approximately 20 minutes, the teacher calls time and all the students go over their review sheets. I like the procedure, and it does seem successful in producing capable spellers.

JANUARY 14, 20—Today I brought two of my pet mice to school. They are a hit! Most of the students are rather apprehensive about them. One boy (Erick) is quite knowledgeable about rodents in general. I now know all the kids by first name. Most of them know my name, too.

JANUARY 17, 20—I followed my class around all day today. We began our day with reading and a handwriting exercise. Then at 9:45 we went to art. From there we went to math. The students went over some sample math exercises involving multiplication and division of small or single-digit numbers and some double-digit numbers. From there we went to social studies where the students were reviewing for a test the following day. After lunch the class went to science; here they were read to by the teacher about electrons and protons. After science the class moved to English. Here, the English teacher had the students write in their journals about "wintertime." Of all the lessons I observed this day, I enjoyed the English lesson best of all. At 1:45 the students went to computer lab, where they could freely choose which program they would like to work with.

Overall, I would say the day was sort of boring—with the exceptions of reading, art, computer, and English. It's no wonder the students go crazy when they get a free moment. They work in each class and have homework in all of them if they fail to complete their in-class assignments. . . .

JANUARY 23–24, 20—The days are running together now. My responsibilities are that of an observer and occasional participant. Most of my participation occurs in reading and computer lab. In reading, the students are all reading for a "Bookit Goal." This is a program done by Pizza Hut. Each month the students must read five books. The teacher verifies this by having the students retell the stories: main character, plot, etc. I listen to the students who have read short stories in their basal reader. They tell me the story. I grill them very thoroughly, demanding to know higher-level associations such as: Why do you think the character chose to respond the way he did?

In computer, the students do drills and exercises. They are then rewarded with some sort of game. They seem really content with this. Yet, am not so sure I really go along with all of it. I think there should be programs that "grade" the students' progress (for example, with multiplication and division). The days are flying fast now. I have been riding my bike to school every day it's not raining. The children are going crazy, wanting to know where I park it. I tell them I have been parking it in the "Bat Cave." I love it, and it's driving them crazy. The kids are great. I am still having a blast. . . .

FEBRUARY 11, 20—The mother mouse had babies. Tiquanna and I predicted the correct number. The children are jazzed up about the mice. I told the students I would be hanging with them for the next 12 weeks. . . .

FEBRUARY 21, 20—So much happens each day. Sometimes I am overwhelmed. It is no wonder teachers burn out. We hit the deck running about 8:00 and don't stop until 2:30. Then we plan and prepare for the next day until 3:30 or so. Tomorrow is a big day. Dr. Arnold is coming by to watch me teach my lesson. I am prepared, yet a little apprehensive. Cindy (Ms. Owenbey) has been letting me do lessons off and on, so the children are aware of my role as their teacher. . . .

FEBRUARY 25, 20—It worked great. I split the children into two groups and had them chorus-read. They struggled with it, but I feel with a little time we will be moving along a lot more smoothly. I emphasized that we are to improve our reading skills by keeping up with the group. They struggled with the activity, but I think they did so because it was novel. Great day!

(The log continues in this manner, with Michael Kealohalan Anderson (called Lani) telling of his observations, his work with small groups and individuals, and his initial teaching experiences.)

Expanding Beyond Observation

School-based observation and teaching experiences are the bridge between the worlds of theory and practice. Throughout your education and psychology programs you will be examining theory: theories about how eight-year-olds learn, about the success of disabled youngsters in the regular classroom, about the best ways to group, about the most effective way to organize a lesson, about how to deal with disruptive students, etc. However, until you have had the opportunity to sit in a classroom and observe what occurs from the teacher's point of view, none of these theories will be real.

While surveying three teacher-preparation programs, Dorothy Sluss and Sam Minner of East Tennessee State University interviewed 26 classroom teachers. One teacher uttered a truism we often apply to teaching children, but frequently forget when teaching adults: "Children learn what they live. So do people who want to be teachers. If you want to learn about children, go where the children are. Don't just read about it in some book" (1999, 283).

Therefore, observation—gaining knowledge and understanding—should come first. Once you have had the opportunity to reflect on the teachers, students, classrooms, and schools that you will observe, as will be discussed in Chapters 2 through 4, you will begin using what you have learned in your own planning and teaching. Pierce calls this kind of learning, "authentic learning" (1996, 217). For many of you, this will begin as early as your first class in education. For others, authentic learning will not occur until much later in your teacher-education program.

Observing a teacher can show you a great deal about how to teach, but it will not tell you how *you* will teach. Educator Philip Jackson at the University of Chicago relates a time when he was a principal and visited several nursery-school classrooms. He noted how teachers bent down to the eye level of children, how they held books on their laps, reading upside down so the children could see. He thought he could probably teach nursery-school. But as he talked to the teachers, he realized that it was more than holding the book, bandaging the knee, and eyeballing the child. It was "seeing/reacting in a certain spirit or manner to a special portion of the world—rooms full of three- and four-year-olds" (1986, 88). According to Jackson, specific skills such as how to make play dough are important, but feeling and acting at home in a particular instructional milieu is essential for a true teacher. Until you have had the experience of teaching, you will not know whether you feel at home with particular students in a particular educational setting.

A good analogy for the importance of early school-based teaching experiences is that of learning to fly an airplane. Initially, student pilots might use flight simulators to experience flying a plane, but very early in their training they take command of the real plane as the instructor watches and critiques. This does not mean the simulator stops serving a function for them. In fact, they will use it many times to simulate uncommon occurrences. However, nothing substitutes for the experience of actually flying the plane. Simulated teaching experiences—role-playing classroom experiences with peers—will continue to be a helpful tool throughout your teacher training. But nothing will substitute for the teacher serving as your evaluator and mentor. As one preservice teacher reported at the end of her observation and participation experience, "We have all heard that experience is the best teacher. I can assure you that is the case with me. I know that I will refer to this experience for many years to come as a constant reminder to learn by doing. I admit I dreaded this experience at first. I would do it again and again, but this time, not for a grade, but for the experience!" (Chance, Morris, and Rakes 1996, 388).

Experience Alone Is Not Always a Good Teacher

Throughout your time observing and participating in the classroom, you will need to make meaning of the events you see and experience. You will gain deeper understanding of student behaviors, teaching styles, and curriculum if you learn to make them meaningful. Researcher Selma Wasserman of Simon Fraser University in British Columbia concludes that making meaning from your field experiences can be more complicated than it appears. Your developmental history, your beliefs, and your values have formed your perceptions. Most likely they will play a part in the way you observe and what you take away from those observations.

Also, factors such as the time of day, your physical and emotional state, personal biases, and your classroom mentor and professor can influence the meaning you derive from your experiences (Wasserman 1999, 466–67).

It is your responsibility to make your observation and participation as meaningful and helpful as possible by collecting data, analyzing it, and reflecting upon it. Throughout your preservice time in the classroom, you will be using techniques such as checklists, anecdotal records, coding, and interviewing. Following the collection of data from these instruments, you will be involved in the process of reflection. Objective data collection and reflective thinking will enable you to gain meaningful information and knowledge about teaching and learning.

For the preservice teacher, teaching and learning should go hand in hand. For example, those who first experience teaching in student-centered classrooms might think the students are off task and out of control if they are not familiar with the student-centered approach. They may come away from this experience saying, "This kind of classroom is not for me." However, if they had first studied the student-centered classroom, observed in one, and examined teaching techniques common in such environments, the experience might have been different. Their conclusions would be based on knowledge rather than on misinterpretations of what they had experienced.

Frequently, novice teachers make incorrect assumptions about the success of lessons they have taught. For example, Hank believed a lesson was successful because the students were well behaved and responsive to his jokes and questions. His conclusion may be misleading. Assume that Hank has spent little or no time preparing the lesson. However, because he is glib and funny, the students are well behaved and appear to respond. Their behavior may have little or nothing to do with the lesson or with Hank. Perhaps the students are exceptionally well behaved. Perhaps the classroom teacher has prepared them for Hank's teaching by telling them they must be on their best behavior, or by rewarding them for good behavior. Hank, like the cat who jumps on the cold stove and assumes it will always be cold, assumes that students will always behave and respond positively to his teaching and that he doesn't need to change anything in his preparation or approach.

This example is also miseducative in that Hank assumes that the only role of the teacher is to deliver lessons. He neglects to see the teacher setting realistic objectives and evaluating students on those objectives. If he continually fails to plan, how will he know what his teaching objectives are? If he has no objectives, how will he know if the students have learned what he's taught?

The Importance of Feedback in Early Teaching Experiences

Nothing is more important than good feedback about initial teaching experiences. Good does not necessarily mean positive. Good feedback for Hank might include a preteaching conference with the classroom teacher, Mr. Thornberg, to discuss the lesson. This conference could lead Hank to develop plans. Mr. Thornberg might ask: What will you be teaching today? What are your objectives for the lesson? How will you ensure the students are progressing toward the objectives? How will you determine if they learned what you taught?

If the preteaching conference does not lead to plan development, the after-teaching conference between Hank and Mr. Thornberg might. Mr. Thornberg tells Hank that he has good rapport with the students. Then he asks these questions: What did you expect the students to learn from your lesson? What methods did you employ to ensure they learned it? How did you involve the students in their own learning? How will you evaluate what they have learned? How will you grade them on what occurred today? If Karen's mother comes in and asks what Karen missed while she was absent, what will you tell her? Hank may now understand that he must do more than perform.

Unfortunately, the feedback that preservice teachers receive can also be miseducative. Most of us want to give positive feedback to our students, and, unlike the situation in an airplane cockpit, positive feedback about teaching is not immediately dangerous. In fact, most teachers have discovered that positive feedback increases motivation and improves results. However, if preservice teachers accept positive feedback as the final truth, they may miss opportunities to gain valuable insight. To avoid this problem, you should always ask teachers who evaluate your classroom performance, "What would you have done differently?"

Overly negative feedback can be just as misleading. Sometimes classroom teachers expect preservice teachers to perform beyond their capabilities. This usually occurs because the classroom teacher is unfamiliar with the preservice teacher's education program. The classroom teacher may not understand that it is the preservice teacher's first class in education, or she may not know that the student is expected to be working only with an individual child. To avoid this problem, the preservice teacher should acquaint the classroom teacher with the role he or she is expected to play. Communication and feedback between preservice teacher, classroom teacher, and university supervisor is essential if the early field experience is to be beneficial. Other suggestions later in this book will help students avoid misunderstandings about roles.

The Importance of Reflective Observation

What is reflection? Why is it so important? And what's the big deal anyway? Although using reflection as a tool to improve learning about teaching is a relatively recent phenomenon, the process of reflection is one that scholars have touted for generations. Philosopher and educator John Dewey wrote in 1910, "Reflection is aimed at the discovery of facts that will serve a purpose." The guiding factor in the process of reflection, according to Dewey, is the "demand for the solution of a perplexity" (Dewey 1910, 1921). So, if we want to solve a problem, we must reflect on it. Educational theorist Jerome Bruner went even further. "Reflection," he said, "is central to all learning" (Bruner 1960, 13). There is hardly a self-help book on the market today that does not mention the importance of reflection. Books that claim to document the attributes of successful people always stress the reflective process that leads an individual to success. Sometime watch the face of an accomplished athlete after he has missed the ball in the end zone or she has fallen from the balance beam; you will see in the athlete's eyes a rapid analysis of what occurred. There may be only a few seconds to reflect on what went wrong, but reflection is necessary so that the same mistake will not occur again. This, of course, is why teams watch videos of the game and performers tape performances. This is what makes greatness. Many people who are "naturals" never become accomplished. Why? They have not learned the skill of reflection. So, too, with teachers. Those who reflect on their actions and performance are more successful than those who merely react.

Is reflection a skill that can be taught and learned? Of course it is. And, once you learn it, like riding a bike, you never lose it. Reflective individuals simply think about what they have seen and done. They gather information and analyze it. Frequently they write down what they have observed, as a way of processing their thoughts. Sometimes they video or audiotape their "performances." Sometimes they talk to themselves and even tape their thoughts. Often they clarify their thinking by talking to others and testing their thoughts. Reflection is at first introspective, but later it becomes active and interactive. Of course, true reflective thinkers choose carefully whom they share their thoughts with—selecting those people who can help them grow in their understanding. At the same time, reflective people continue the introspective process while they are actively pursing information and clarification. Reflection is not difficult. Often it merely requires answering simple questions: What did I do? How do I feel? Why do I feel that way? What was the best thing that happened? Were there any things I could have done better? What would I do differently if I could do it again? Sometime these questions are processed in a matter of seconds, such as with the gymnast who must immediately return to the balance beam. Other times the process is deliberate and slow. These simple questions, whether processed quickly or with deliberance, will lead you to become a reflective thinker.

FIGURE 1.1

The Reflection Cycle

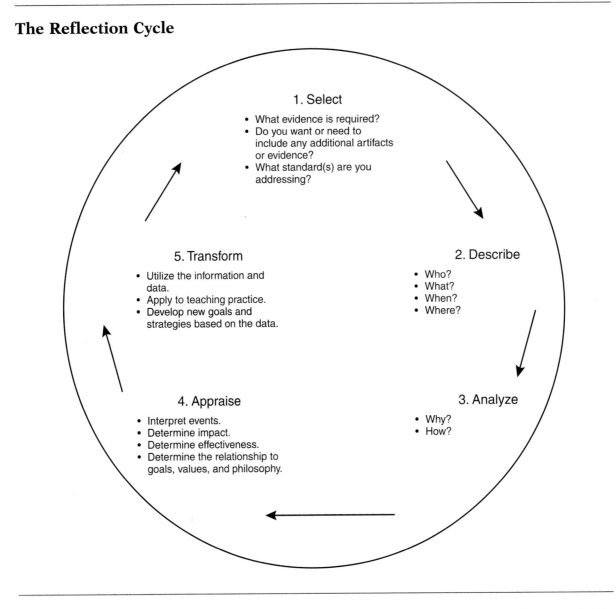

Source: Adapted from the Administrator Appraisal System Institute, North Carolina Department of Public Instruction, *Performance-Based Licensure*, 1998–1999.

The Reflection Process

Becoming a reflective practitioner requires time, practice, and an environment supportive to the development and organization of the reflection process. This is a highly individualized process, and each individual should find the structure and method of reflection that best suits him or her. This includes answering these questions: When is the best time for me to reflect on what I have learned and experienced? Where will I be most comfortable reflecting? Do I need any tools to help me in the process, such as a computer, a journal, copies of lessons, etc.?

The reflective process itself can be seen as a series of steps known as the reflection cycle (see Figure 1.1). Although at first this cycle may seem complex, when you learn to utilize it

FIGURE 1.2

Writing a Reflection

Select: What evidence/artifacts have you included?

Describe: This step involves a description of the circumstances, situations, or issues related to the evidence or artifact. Four "W" questions are usually addressed:

- Who was involved?
- What were the circumstances, concerns, or issues?
- When did the event occur?
- Where did the event occur?

Analyze: This step involves "digging deeper." The "Why" of the evidence or artifact and the "How" of its relationship to your teaching practice should be addressed.

Appraise: In the previous three steps, you have described and analyzed an experience, a piece of evidence, or an activity. The actual self-assessment occurs at this stage as you interpret the activity or evidence and evaluate its appropriateness and impact.

Transform: This step holds the greatest opportunity for growth as you use the insights gained from reflection in improving and transforming your practice.

Source: Adapted from the Administrator Appraisal System Institute, North Carolina Department of Public Instruction, *Performance-Based Licensure*, 1998–1999.

you can reach a solution to a problem on the spot. It can also be used at a quiet time when you have the luxury to really think through a complex set of circumstances. The goal of this cycle is not to dictate how you will reflect on what you observe or experience in the classroom, but rather as a beginning place in the development of your own reflective process.

Writing a Reflection

To help you become a reflective practitioner, it is necessary to practice the process of reflection. As with most people, it may be a good idea for you to begin by writing your reflections in a journal, a notebook, or in a special file in your computer documents. Figure 1.2 shows a series of suggested steps for writing a reflection related to your classroom observation or experience.

PART II

Observing in the Schools

Chapter Two
Observing Teachers

Effective observation is a process of "selective watching." This means the observation should have both an objective and a procedure of what to look for (Duckett 1980, 1). We all know the story of several people watching the same fender bender and each seeing a totally different accident. Why does this occur? The answer is simple. What we see is based on our experiences, values, and beliefs. Hence, if observation is to be effective in the learning process, it must be objective. To be objective, observation requires structure. You must have a plan, an objective, and a guide to follow. In addition, you must plan ahead. You need to be so aware of exactly what you are looking for that you can see it even when dozens of other things have the potential of distracting you. Think for a minute about the typical classroom. How many things are occurring at any given time? Dozens. Hundreds. Julio is shifting around in his seat. Sara is sharpening her pencil. A poster falls off the wall. Kenya is asking a question. Ten students are raising their hands. Marquette is at the teacher's desk listing the names of those students who have paid for the field trip. Mr. Lazaro is putting the assignment on the board. You get the idea. Unless you know what you are looking for, how can you find it?

The carefully developed and field-tested observation instruments in this guide will assist you in completing objective observations that are effective in helping you learn about teaching. By utilizing the observation instruments, you will maximize the usefulness of the hours you spend in classroom observation and participation.

Observing in Classrooms

One important technique for learning about effective teaching is observing capable teachers at work in their classrooms. Observing is a skill that needs to be developed in order to yield the best results. As education professors and authors Michael Morehead and David Cropp suggest, "Observation which is conducted by the preservice teacher without the benefit of a prescribed structure . . . may not assist in the development of a future teacher" (1994, 2). One needs to know what to look for, how to look for it, and how to be objective in one's analysis.

In the following excerpts, two university students observe the same teacher in a second-grade classroom. Note how, in their analyses, they come to different conclusions.

Sarah's Observation Log

As soon as the bell rang the children moved quietly to their seats. They seemed to know exactly what to do, exactly what was expected of them. They put their books in their desks and folded their hands on top of the desks as Mrs. Menotti instructed the two class monitors to collect the lunch and the picture money. She reminded them to have the students check off their names on the list when the money was turned in. As the students did this, Mrs. Menotti read the morning announcements. All the time she read,

15

she was monitoring the students collecting the money. There were no disruptions, and the students seemed to collect the money in an orderly fashion. She did not call the roll, but I saw her put the attendance slip on the outside of the classroom door. Because the children have assigned seats, she could simply look to see who was not present. All of this was accomplished in less than ten minutes.

Mrs. Menotti told the children she would meet first with the red reading group in the reading circle. The other children would find their assignments on the board written in the color of their reading group. What a great idea! I'll have to remember this one. The children quietly took out their books, and all but two began to work while Mrs. Menotti was telling the reading group what to do. When she looked up and saw one child not working and another talking to the child next to him, she went to the board and wrote their names on it. The children immediately got to work.

Although I couldn't really hear the reading group, I could see the flip chart on which Mrs. Menotti had written letter combinations that would be used in the story. I could tell that each child was reading round-robin fashion, and that Mrs. Menotti interrupted only when a child needed help sounding out a word.

Since the rest of the class was working quietly in their workbooks, I took this time to look at the classroom. I was impressed with how neat and organized it was. All the desks were in neat rows. In the right front of the room was the reading circle. Mrs. Menotti sat so that she could see the children in the circle as well as the rest of the room. On the walls were colorful posters. The bookshelves were very carefully organized. On the bulletin board behind Mrs. Menotti's desk was a neat display of student work, which was very nicely done. There was an overhead projector in the front of the room. Also there were maps and a globe. There were lots of dictionaries and books in the book cabinets. There were no papers on the floor, and the children kept their books in their desks. Mrs. Menotti kept the shades drawn most of the way down so the children were not distracted.

Only once during the reading group did Mrs. Menotti have to stop to reprimand a student. It was one of the same students as earlier, and she went to the board to put a check next to his name and reminded him that it was not art time and he shouldn't be drawing and should be working in his workbook. He put his drawing in his desk, and I noticed that he did not concentrate on his workbook, but instead doodled around the edge of the page. At one point, I noticed that he was doing his drawing inside his desk. Mrs. Menotti did not seem to notice, and I wondered if I should have told her.

After about twenty minutes, the reading groups changed in an orderly fashion. The blue group went to the reading circle, and the red group took out their books and began doing the assignments written in red on the board.

I was really impressed with the order and organization in this classroom. Almost all of the students were quiet and actively involved in their work. Mrs. Menotti was able to work with the few students in the reading group. I hope I can have such an orderly classroom some day.

Steve's Observation Log

That same morning, Steve observed in Mrs. Menotti's classroom. Here are some excerpts from his observation log:

I got to the classroom about ten minutes before the bell rang. I introduced myself to Mrs. Menotti. Although she seemed friendly and told me to make myself at home, I had the feeling that she was distracted and rather cool. The children were having a wonderful time talking and giggling in small groups. The boys in the group nearest to me were talking about the soccer game. They were really excited that they had won. I already knew that I'd like these children. They were enthusiastic, bright-eyed, and bushy-tailed.

When the bell rang, everything changed. The atmosphere became rigid. Mrs. Menotti stood in the front of the room, staring at the class. She didn't say anything, but her message was clear: "It's time to get to work." The students stopped talking and moved to their desks, which were in rigid rows. Mrs. Menotti never smiled or said "Good morning." She just told the two monitors to collect lunch and picture money as she read the announcements. I noticed that the students selected as monitors appeared to be upper-class students in expensive-looking clothes. While they were taking the money, one of them seemed to be giving some of the less-well-dressed children a hard time, but Mrs. Menotti had not seemed to notice. Since the children's seats seemed to be assigned, she took attendance without calling roll. Although the class was orderly, it seemed as if the children might as well not have been there. The only ones Mrs. Menotti called by name were the monitors. I think my first impression was right: Mrs. Menotti is a very cold woman.

I couldn't help but notice how cold the classroom was. The only work of the children that was displayed was behind Mrs. M.'s desk, where the children can't go easily. It looked like perfect penmanship papers to me. The only other decorations in the room were mass-marketed posters that looked like they'd been here since Mrs. M. started teaching twenty years ago. The shades were down, and the only light in the room was artificial. I would hate to be a student here, and my sense was that the children didn't much like it either. I hadn't seen one smile since the bell rang.

When it was time to go to reading group, Mrs. Menotti called the red group to the circle. Is this class ability-grouped? I think so. It looked like all the children in the red group were wearing designer clothes. The two monitors were in that group. When they got in the group, Mrs. M. noticed two boys who had not yet started to work in their workbooks. It seemed that one boy couldn't read the assignment on the board, and I can understand why. He was in the yellow group, so the assignment was written in yellow and hard to see from where he sat. However, Mrs. M. didn't ask why he was talking; she just put his name on the board. I noticed a tear in his eye. I was beginning to dislike Mrs. Menotti. Another boy was fussing in his desk. He didn't seem to be able to find his book, so his name went on the board, too.

I watched the reading group for about ten minutes, and it looked deadly. Mrs. Menotti had letter combinations on the flip chart. As the children read in order she pointed to the letters and asked them to make the sound. It seemed to me that the children read very well and did not need this kind of instruction. Since I was bored I decided to walk around to see what kind of seatwork the kids were doing. Each group seemed to be working on a different page in the same workbook. I can tell who the "smart" kids are. They can tell, too. At one point, Mrs. Menotti stopped the reading group to yell at the same boy who could not see the board earlier. He was still not doing his work. I noticed earlier that he was drawing, and he is a really good artist. But, she does not acknowledge his ability. Instead his name got a check, and she told him he could come in after school to do his seatwork. So much for the value of art in this classroom!

It's no wonder so many kids drop out of school before they graduate. Mrs. Menotti has already decided that Shane, the artist, will be one of them. What hopes are there for Shane?

Conclusion. Both Sarah and Steve observed the same class during the same period of time; each saw a totally different Mrs. Menotti from a radically different perspective. Sarah's Mrs. Menotti was well organized, and the classroom environment was conducive to work and study. Steve's Mrs. Menotti distanced herself from the students, and the environment was controlled and nonproductive. How could two students from the same university class see such different things in the identical classroom?

Effective Observation

Most simply, observation is the act or practice of paying attention to people, events, and/or the environment. The difficulty with observation is that every individual brings to an event his or her psychological perception of it.

However, not all observation is subjective. It also can occur systematically and be conducted fairly objectively. The fact that Sarah and Steve were required to observe in Mrs. Menotti's classroom means that the observation was deliberate, and, therefore, more formalized than everyday observation. However, it was not systematic. Systematic observation is long-term observation involving visiting a classroom many times and observing many different situations. It is planned, objective, and goal or question oriented. The observers identify beforehand what they are looking for and how they will carry it out. This is known as "targeted observation" (Yapp and Young 1999, 27). Sarah and Steve's observations were not targeted. Thus, their observations may simply have reinforced their existing prejudices, thereby "arresting or distorting the growth from further experiences" (Evertson and Green 1986, 95).

Objectivity in Observation. Because teachers and classrooms are so different, observation can be difficult. If the observer tries to do more than record exactly what he or she sees, the conclusions will be filtered through his or her prejudices and biases.

The goal of the systematic observer, then, is to gather as much data as possible over a period of several observations about the classroom, the students, the teacher, and the curriculum. Pierce states that in order for observations to be of practical use, "they must be structured and focused on specific events that the students have been well prepared to identify and analyze" (1996, 218). The more data that are identified and analyzed, the easier it will be to get a complete picture. The methods of obtaining as objective a point of view as possible involve anecdotal observation, structured observation, and interview. The goal of this chapter is to help you develop as a teacher by providing you with objective, systematic observation tools and techniques as the beginning step to learning how effective teachers teach. In subsequent chapters, you will find tools for objective observations of classrooms, schools, students, and curriculum.

Techniques of Observation. Anecdotal observations focus on the situation and specifically on who says or does what rather than on personalities or interpretations of events. Structured observations are formal and require that observers look for and record specified information that is called for on such things as checklists, sociograms, and profiles. The interview is a technique that seeks to find information through direct questioning. This method can be extremely valuable in understanding a procedure one has observed or the rationale behind it. The interview must be planned for and conducted as objectively as possible.

Anecdotal Observation

Anecdotal observations focus on exactly what occurs in a classroom or on what a child does or says in a specific situation over a limited period of time. Anecdotal observations are informally recorded in narrative in an observer's observation log. As much as possible, they are an exact description of a classroom event or incident. Anecdotal observations are simple to do. Observers need no training, but must follow the rules of all objective observation: (1) the observer must observe the entire sequence or event, (2) goals, limits, or guidelines must be set, (3) the observation should be recorded completely and carefully, and (4) observation must be as objective as possible.

Observing the Entire Event or Sequence

Typically, anecdotal observations deal with what might be called minimal situations. The observer watches one child or one teaching or management technique for a specified period of time over several observations. This observation allows the observer to make dated notes while focusing attention on a single element or individual in the classroom or school. The minimal situation technique narrows the observer's focus to one event. Trying to follow too many elements of the classroom at one time usually leads to incomplete observation of all of them. Focusing on too much caused Sarah and Steve to make inaccurate judgments.

SAMPLE FORM 1

Anecdotal Record Form for Observing Teachers or Instructional Events—1

NAME OF OBSERVER: Karen Susan Richie

DATE AND TIME OF OBSERVATION: December 2, 20—, 10:30 a.m.

LENGTH OF OBSERVATION: Approximately 35 minutes

PERSON AND/OR EVENT OBSERVED: Mrs. Menotti teaching a reading lesson

GRADE LEVEL AND/OR SUBJECT: Second grade; reading

OBJECTIVE OF OBSERVATION: To determine how Mrs. Menotti works with individuals within the reading group

Instructions to the Observer: As completely and accurately as possible, describe the person or the event. If appropriate, include direct quotes and descriptions of the location or individual. Try to avoid making judgments.

Mrs. Menotti called the red group, the Space Invaders, to the reading corner at the right rear of the classroom. "Be sure to bring your free reading books with you, Space Invaders," said Mrs. M.

I moved over to the reading corner so I could better observe the group. The reading corner was next to the window and the students' chairs were arranged in a circle. Mrs. M.'s chair was a large, wooden-slat rocking chair next to the bookcase. Her chair was in the circle of chairs.

The students got their books from their desks. Joey said, "Mrs. M., I finished my book, and I need to see if I can find it in the library." "Is it in the classroom library, Joey?" Mrs. M. asked. "Yes," "O.K., you can look for it, Joey. Just don't disturb the rest of us while you're looking."

Once all the students (except Joey) were seated in the circle, Mrs. M. took out her own book. She said to Joey, "Have you found it?" "Not yet," Joey replied. "Well, join us while I read, and you can go back to the library and look afterward."

Mrs. M. asked Melody if she could remember what happened last in the story. (I couldn't see the title of the book Mrs. M. was reading from. I must remember to ask her.)

continued

Melody began to tell the story. She talked so quietly that it was difficult to hear her. Mrs. M. asked the other students some questions. "Sandy, can you remember what happened to the rabbit when the boy got sick?" "They took him from the nursery," Sandy said. "They were afraid the rabbit was comintated [sic]," said Maggie. "Do you mean 'contaminated'?" asked Mrs. M. Maggie looked at her hands. "Yes," said Maggie very quietly. "Very good, Maggie. That's right," said Mrs. M. Maggie looked up and smiled. "Why do you think they were afraid the rabbit might be contaminated, Sean?" Sean replied, "Well, he was stuffed and the boy is real sick, so the rabbit might have germs." "Very good, Sean," said Mrs. M.

She began to read. All the students were listening. After each page she showed the children the illustration on the page. She read one page and turned to the next and Sean said, "Hey, Mrs. M., you forgot to show us the picture." "There isn't one on that page, Sean."

She read for about ten minutes and asked, "Do you like the story, Abbie?" Abbie nodded her head. "Why do you like it?" she asked. "I like the boy and I want him to get well and get his rabbit back. It's sad," said Abbie. "Do you like sad stories, Mark?" "Yes, sometimes," said Mark. "Is the story you've been reading sad?" "No," Mark said. "Would you tell us about your book, Mark, please?" Mark did. It's the story of a space trip to Mars taken by a little boy. Melody said, "Did he really take that trip, Mark? I think it was all a dream." "No," said Mark, "It was real." "How do you know, Mark?" asked Sean. Mark said back very loudly, "Because the book doesn't say it's a dream." "Yeah," said Melody, "but in the beginning of the book he's in bed, and in the end he's back in his bed." Mark was quiet. Mrs. M. smiled, "When you read a story you can decide for yourself what it means. If Melody thinks it was a dream, that's O.K., even if Mark doesn't think it's a dream. Why don't you read it, Melody, and see if you still think it's a dream." Melody did not answer. Mrs. M. turned to Joey and said, "Joey, do you want to get your book so that you can tell us about it after Abbie tells us about hers?"

(Karen's observation continues until the reading group is over.)

Setting Goals, Limits, or Guidelines

As with all observation, the observer must know the objective of the observation. What is it the observer hopes to see in the classroom or school? The observer may simply want to explore how the teacher communicates with individual students, as Karen observed in this sample anecdotal record form for observing teachers. Another way is to keep a simple anecdotal record of student-teacher communication. The observer writes as accurately as possible all the communication that occurs between the teacher and one student during a specified period of time. Since one important element of an effective school is good communication, examining how the teacher communicates with individual students can reveal a great deal about whether or not the classroom is effective. Of course, several observations of this student and other students would be required before a judgment could be made.

SAMPLE FORM 2

Anecdotal Teacher-Student Interaction Form

NAME OF OBSERVER: Karen Susan Richie

DATE AND TIME OF OBSERVATION: December 2, 20—, 10:30 a.m.

LENGTH OF OBSERVATION: Approximately 35 minutes

TEACHER: Mrs. Menotti

STUDENT: Joey

GRADE LEVEL AND/OR SUBJECT: Second grade

OBJECTIVE OF OBSERVATION: How does Mrs. Menotti interact with an individual student?

Instructions to the Observer: As completely and accurately as possible, describe the interactions between the teacher and one selected student. Include direct quotes and descriptions of the teacher and the student, including facial expressions, gestures, and voice quality. However, be careful to avoid making judgments.

Time	Teacher	Student
10:36	Mrs. Menotti	**JOEY** "Mrs. M., I finished my book, and I need to see if I can find it in the library." Joey called out very loudly across the room to Mrs. M.
	Mrs. M. smiled at Joey and made a "sh" sign. She looked him directly in the eye, "Is it in the classroom library, Joey?"	
		"Yes." Joey answered much more quietly and smiled back at Mrs. M.
	"O.K. you can look for it, Joey. Just don't disturb the rest of us while you're looking."	
		Joey moved quietly to the classroom library behind Mrs. M's rocking chair and began to search.

Perhaps the observer might want to examine another element of an effective school: rewarding student achievement. The observer might use the anecdotal recording technique to determine how the teacher and the school reward the students for academic achievement. To do this, the observer simply examines the classroom and the school building for signs that student achievement has been rewarded and lists those in the observation log.

SAMPLE FORM 3

Anecdotal Record Form for Observing Teachers or Instructional Events—2

NAME OF OBSERVER: James McClure

DATE AND TIME OF OBSERVATION: January 6, 20—, 9:35 a.m.

LENGTH OF OBSERVATION: 30 minutes

PERSON AND/OR EVENT OBSERVED: Mr. Martine's classroom

GRADE LEVEL AND/OR SUBJECT: Eighth grade; language arts and social studies

OBJECTIVE OF OBSERVATION: To determine how school/classroom environment promotes student achievement

Instructions to the Observer: As completely and accurately as possible, describe the person or the event. If appropriate, include direct quotes and descriptions of the location or the individual. Try to avoid making judgments.

1. Student work displayed on bulletin boards in hallways.

2. Students who won speech contest mentioned over intercom during morning announcements.

3. Teacher mentioned a student who won a Boy Scout honor.

4. Classroom bulletin board displayed students' writing from last week.

5. Students were working on putting together a desktop computer publication of their writing.

6. Books children have written and illustrated were on check-out shelf at the rear of the room.

7. Student artwork related to social studies unit was displayed on the wall above the windows.

Recording Completely and Carefully

Anecdotal records require carefully recording events over a specified period of time. It might be useful for the observer to do two or more recordings, since it is impossible to write down everything that occurs in just one observation. For example, in observing one child, he might record the child's activities every five minutes for an hour. Later he might record her activities every five minutes for another hour. It is important for the observer to write down exactly what the child is doing, avoiding any judgments of her behavior. A schedule is also important if the goal of the observer is to examine classroom organization. For example, if an observer is watching grouping techniques in a classroom, she might record the formal and informal grouping patterns every thirty minutes. An anecdotal observation like this reveals an interesting grouping pattern in Mr. Hanks's classroom that observation of everything in the classroom might not.

SAMPLE FORM 4

Anecdotal Record Form for Grouping Patterns

NAME OF OBSERVER: Sylvia Rodriguez

DATE AND TIME OF OBSERVATION: October 29, 20—, 8:45 a.m.

LENGTH OF OBSERVATION: All day

PERSON AND/OR EVENT OBSERVED: Mr. Hanks

GRADE LEVEL AND/OR SUBJECT: Fifth grade

OBJECTIVE OF OBSERVATION: To examine grouping patterns

Instructions to the Observer: As completely and accurately as possible, describe the different groups in the classroom. If appropriate, include direct quotes and descriptions of locations or individuals. Try to avoid making judgments.

8:45   Reading groups met with teacher; all of the children in each group read in turn from the same-level basal reader; three different level readers were used by the five groups. The teacher reinforced skills by calling the children's attention to words on a flip chart.

9:15   Math groups in which all the children were working on different kinds of math problems; two groups were doing long division, another multiplication, another fractions (population of the math groups differs from population of the reading groups—i.e., Sarah Jane is in the fraction math group, but was reading from the lowest-level reader).

9:45   Children continued in math groups; three larger groups divided into pairs; the pairs were helping each other complete the homework assignments listed for each group on the chalkboard.

       Mr. Hanks spent all his time working with the multiplication group—the only group not working in pairs—except for a few minutes to answer the questions of the other groups.

10:15   Recess—children formed their own groups: a group of ten boys was playing soccer, a group of seven girls was skipping rope, two girls were reading, a group of four boys was playing chase, two girls were walking, one girl was sitting with Mr. Hanks.

10:45   Social studies groups—students were investigating different aspects of the community. The children seemed to know their assignments; each student had a folder which was picked up at the front of the room when Mr. Hanks announced it was time for social studies; the students went to the supply cabinet or the bookshelves when they needed materials; they went up to Mr. Hanks's desk with questions. (Mr. Hanks did not work with these groups, but observed their activities from his desk.)

11:45   Lunch (did not observe).

12:00   All students participated in a class meeting with Mr. Hanks about the Halloween party (the class president presided over this large group); students sat in a large circle; they raised their hands when they wanted to make a point; Mr. Hanks recorded each point made on a flip chart; he only spoke to redirect the discussion to other students.

continued

12:30   Students lined up by row, as called by Mr. Hanks, to go to music; one row of mostly boys was not allowed to leave until they quieted down; they did not have their materials put away and were busy talking; it took about three minutes for them to get organized and quiet; then Mr. Hanks let them leave.

2:15   Small groups participated in a variety of classroom management chores (i.e., one group picked up papers and cleaned desks, tables, and floor; another group rearranged the chairs and adjusted the blinds; a third group put papers in students' folders; a fourth group collected books and placed them on the bookshelves).

Structured Observations

Structured observations follow a specific format. As in anecdotal observations, one should follow the rules of objective observation. Unlike anecdotal observations, structured observations are formal and require that specific information be recorded. Structured observations include rank ordering, coding, checklists, interviews (discussed in this chapter), profiles, and sociograms (discussed in Chapter 4).

Rank Ordering

One easy, nonjudgmental way to examine what has been observed in the classroom is to organize the observations in order of frequency. Many things can be rank ordered. For example, it is possible to rank order the following techniques employed by the teacher: instructional techniques (lecturing, discussion, small group work, individual work, etc.), grouping patterns, management approaches, methods of discipline, types of questions, and types of assignments. If Karen—the observer from the sample anecdotal record form for observing teachers or instructional events—had been observing grouping patterns in Mrs. Menotti's classroom over the period of a *week*, she could have rank ordered the grouping patterns by frequency of occurrence. To do this, of course, she would first have to know what types of groups she had seen.

SAMPLE FORM 5

Observation Form for Rank Ordering

NAME OF OBSERVER: Karen Susan Richie

DATE AND TIME OF OBSERVATION: Week of November 4, 20—

LENGTH OF OBSERVATION: One week

TECHNIQUES OR TYPES OBSERVED: Mrs. Menotti—Grouping Patterns

GRADE LEVEL AND/OR SUBJECT: Second grade

OBJECTIVE OF OBSERVATION: To examine grouping patterns

Instructions to the Observer: List a variety of possible techniques or types of grouping patterns. Keep a tally of those you observe. At the end of the observation period, count the number of occurrences of each technique or type.

Techniques or Types of Grouping Patterns	Number of Occurrences
Homogeneous grouping for skills	10
Interest grouping	7
Management grouping	5
Groups based on book read	3
Groups for completing project	2
Total Number of Groups (Week of November 4, 20—)	27

To gain additional insight into the grouping patterns used in Mrs. Menotti's classroom, the percentage of times particular types of grouping patterns were used might be interesting. For example, 37 percent of the groups in Mrs. Menotti's classroom were homogeneous skill groups, and 26 percent were based on interest.

Coding Systems

A coding system is another simple, structured tool for observing in the classroom. A coding system looks for specific elements of teacher and/or student behavior. The observer usually records these elements at a specific interval, or simply tallies the number of times the particular behavior occurs. To complete a coding observation, an observer needs a list of specified behaviors. In this chapter we will provide two types of coding systems: one based on Ned Flanders's student and teacher interactions system, the second based on Norris Sanders's system of questioning. In the first type of coding, the observer records the interaction during a specific interval.

Observing Student-Teacher Interaction. In each of the teacher-student interaction examples, the observer tallies the number of times the following nine categories of interaction between the teacher and students occur.

The first four types of interaction, according to Flanders, show an **indirect teacher influence:**

1. **Accepts feelings**—The teacher accepts or acknowledges student-expressed feelings/concerns in a nonthreatening manner (For example, *Student:* "I don't understand the assignment." *Teacher:* "It is a difficult concept to grasp, isn't it?").

2. **Praises and encourages**—The teacher gives positive evaluation of a student contribution. (For example, *Teacher:* "That's an especially good paper, Sammy.").

3. **Accepts or uses ideas of student**—The teacher clarifies, develops, or refers to a student contribution, usually without evaluation (For example, *Student:* "The electoral college decides which presidential candidate is elected." *Teacher:* "And, the electoral college awards its votes based on the popular vote in each state.").

4. **Asks questions**—The teacher solicits information or asks opinions with the intent that a student answers (For example, *Teacher:* "What is one fact about the electoral college?").

The next three types of student-teacher interaction are considered to be **direct teacher influences:**

5. **Lectures**—The teacher presents ideas, information, or orientation. Lecturing includes rhetorical questions.

6. **Gives directions**—The teacher directs or suggests in a way which indicates that the student is expected to comply (For example, *Teacher:* "Turn to page 72 and complete exercise B.").

7. **Criticizes or justifies authority**—The teacher evaluates a student's contribution negatively or refers to the teacher's authoritative position (For example, *Teacher:* "No, George, the electoral college is not a college for engineers. Where are the notes you took yesterday on this? You know it is your responsibility to take notes in class every day.").

The following two responses fall under the heading of **student talk:**

8. **Student talk-response**—The student directly answers the teacher's question. The answer is usually responsive to the question (For example, *Teacher:* "What is one fact about the electoral college?" *Student:* "The electoral college decides which presidential candidate is elected.").

9. **Student talk-initiation**—The student initiates a comment or question that is unpredictable and/or creative in content (For example, *Student:* "We didn't discuss this yesterday, but I know that eleven presidents won the election by winning the electoral college votes even though they lost the popular vote.").

SAMPLE FORM 6

Coding System—Type and Tally of Student-Teacher Interaction

NAME OF OBSERVER: Eric Dreibholz

DATE AND TIME OF OBSERVATION: December 16, 20—, 2:15 p.m.

LENGTH OF OBSERVATION: 1 hour

ELEMENT OBSERVED: Teacher-student interaction

TEACHER AND/OR STUDENT: Mrs. Rodriguez

GRADE LEVEL AND/OR SUBJECT: Sixth grade; social studies (Civil War)

OBJECTIVE OF OBSERVATION: To examine types of indirect and direct teacher interaction with students and type of student talk in one lesson

Instructions to the Observer: Tally the number of times each interactive behavior occurs during your observation period. Try to record at least one example of each type of interaction. At the end of the observation period, total the number of all teacher-student interactions, and calculate the percentage of the total for each interaction.

Type of Interactive Behavior	Tally of Times Observed	Percentage
INDIRECT		
Accepts Feelings **Example:** "I know some of you don't feel well. You may be discouraged, but let's keep trying."	##	8%
Praises/Encourages **Example:** "I like what you're saying." "Good." "Can you tell us more?"	## ///	12%
Accepts or Uses Student Ideas **Example:** "Nick said General Lee was an outstanding leader—let's talk about that."	////	7%
Asks Questions **Example:** "Why do you think General Lee surrendered at that time?" "What was the turning point of the war?"	## ## ///	21%
DIRECT		
Lectures **Example:** Gave background of Gettysburg Address	///	5%
Gives Directions **Example:** "Think about this question." "Answer questions 1–6 on page 97."	## //	11%
Criticizes or Justifies Authority **Example:** "I don't like the way you crumbled your paper."	///	5%
STUDENT TALK		
Student Talk-Response **Example:** Students answered all directed questions in one or two words or with deeper explanations.	## ## ///	21%
Student Talk-Initiation **Example:** "I agree with Tom, but I think Lee should have waited longer before he surrendered."	## /	10%
TOTALS	62	100%
MOST FREQUENTLY USED TYPE OF INTERACTION	Accepts or uses student ideas and student talk-response.	

Source: Adapted from Ned Flanders, 1985.

Observing Questioning Techniques

There are many approaches for examining questions asked by teachers. A coding system can help observers examine the types of questions asked. We will focus on a technique developed by Norris Sanders (see Table 2.1), based on the cognitive taxonomy of Benjamin Bloom. Bloom's cognitive taxonomy assumes that development of cognitive ability is hierarchical. In other words, understanding of concepts progresses from simple understanding, what

TABLE 2.1

Examples of Levels of Questions Based on Sanders and Bloom

1. **Memory**

   How much is . . . ?
   Who is . . . ?
   What was . . . ?
   When was . . . ?
   Outline the chapter.

2. **Translation**

   What does the definition say?
   What is the English translation of that passage?
   Look on page 27; what does your text say about . . . ?
   Draw a picture of the character in the story we read.

3. **Interpretation**

   In your own words, what does that passage mean?
   Without looking at your text, what is meant by . . . ?
   Write a sentence using the vocabulary word . . .
   Explain the meaning of the graph.
   What is the word problem asking you to do?
   Estimate the number of votes needed to win.

4. **Application**

   What would happen if . . . ?
   What would you do in a similar situation?
   How would you solve that problem?
   Using this play as a model, write your own play based on the story we read.
   Solve the word problem.
   Diagram the . . .
   Demonstrate . . .

5. **Analysis**

   Compare this story to that story.
   Contrast this battle to that battle.
   What was the effect of his decision?
   What caused the problem?
   Is this story based on fact or opinion?
   What is the major theme of the novel?
   What conclusion would you derive from the following . . . ?

6. **Synthesis**

   Write an essay about . . .
   Write an original short story.
   Design your own experiment.
   Using all you have learned about oil painting and portraiture, paint a portrait in oils.
   Develop solutions for the problem of . . .
   Write a computer program.

7. **Evaluation**

   Write a critique of the novel . . .
   Evaluate the quality of . . .
   Argue the following point . . .
   Debate . . .
   Write a point-counterpoint paper on . . .
   Based on all you have learned, evaluate your own work.
   Whose solution proved the most effective?

Bloom calls knowledge or recall (Sanders calls this memory), and comprehension (Sanders calls this translation and interpretation) to more complex knowledge. Bloom labels these higher levels of cognition as analysis, synthesis, and evaluation. In between the less and more complex levels of understanding is the ability to apply (application) one's knowledge to problems and new situations. Bloom's cognitive taxonomy is diagrammed in Figure 2.1. As the chart shows, knowledge is cyclical. Once high levels of knowledge of a concept are achieved, an individual must begin to add to this knowledge by developing new concepts.

Sanders, using Bloom's taxonomy, identifies seven levels of questions, from least to most complex.

1. **Memory:** The student recalls or recognizes information.

2. **Translation:** The student changes information into a different symbolic form or language.

3. **Interpretation:** The student discovers relationships among facts, generalizations, definitions, values, and skills.

4. **Application:** The student solves a real-life problem that requires identification of the issue and the selection and use of appropriate generalizations and skills.

5. **Analysis:** The student solves a problem in the light of conscious knowledge of the parts and forms of thinking.

6. **Synthesis:** The student solves a problem that requires original, creative thinking.

7. **Evaluation:** The student makes a judgment of good or bad, right or wrong, according to standards he designates (Sanders 1966, 3).

If you compare Sanders's levels of questions to Bloom's taxonomy, you will note a few minor differences. Sanders calls the lowest level of questioning *memory* rather than *recall*, as it is designated by Bloom. And Sanders divides the second level of the domain, *comprehension*, into two levels of questions: *translation* and *interpretation*.

To recognize the level of question asked, the observer must be able to examine the question and place it at the appropriate level. The best way to do this is to list all questions asked by the teacher, oral and written, and examine them based on examples of each level provided in Table 2.1. The observer can also use the verbs provided in the central circle of Bloom's cognitive domain in Figure 2.1 to identify the level of a question. The use of a cassette recorder is very helpful in this process. The student observer is cautioned simply to list or record the questions without attempting the examination process until each question asked can be carefully compared with sample questions. It is important to note that if two observers listen to the same lesson, it is likely that even if the questions are identically recorded, the observers' placement of them within levels will differ to some extent.

Since most educators, including Bloom and Sanders, agree that too many lower-level questions (memory, translation, interpretation) and not enough higher-level questions (application, analysis, synthesis, evaluation) are asked, it is helpful to note the frequency of the type of question asked. Observers should keep in mind, however, that in a well-planned lesson, the level of questions asked will directly relate to the teacher's objective for the students. For example, if the teacher's objective is, "The students will examine the feud in *Romeo and Juliet*," it is likely that the questions will be at the lower levels. If however, the objective is, "The students will compare and contrast the feud in *Romeo and Juliet* with other literary and nonliterary feuds," the questions will move from memory to analysis.

FIGURE 2.1

Cognitive Behaviors and Verbs*
Based on Bloom's Cognitive Domain

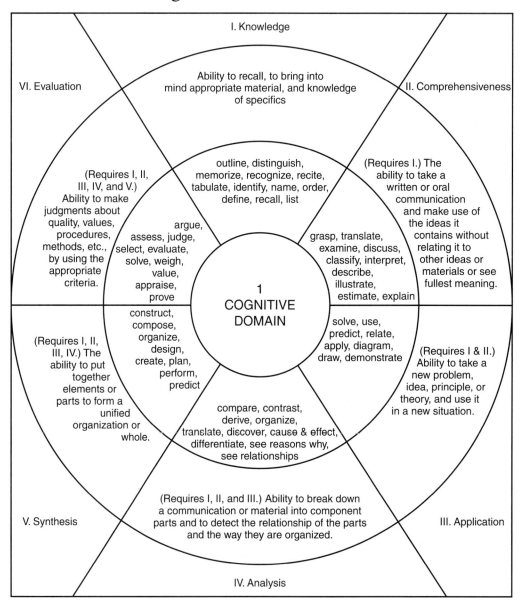

This diagram identifies and explains the six levels of cognitive behaviors; it also gives a sample list of verbs that may be used in relating behavioral objective evaluation to the proper level of cognitive behavior.

*Adapted by Sanchon S. Funk, Jeffrey L. Hoffman, Anne Keithley, and Bruce E. Long of the Florida State University Office of Field Experiences from Benjamin Bloom et al. (ed.), *Taxonomy of Education Objectives: Cognitive Domain*, Longman S. Green and Company, Inc., 1985.

SAMPLE FORM 7

Observation Form for Examining Questions

NAME OF OBSERVER: Ramon Auenida

DATE AND TIME OF OBSERVATION: December 11, 20—, 1:15 p.m.

TEACHER: Mr. Cortines

GRADE LEVEL AND/OR SUBJECT: Tenth grade; science—"The Characteristics of Life"

OBJECTIVE OF OBSERVATION: To examine the level of questions asked by Mr. Cortines

Instructions to the Observer: On a separate piece of paper or on a cassette, record all questions asked by the teacher, orally and in writing, for one lesson. Then place each question below at the appropriate level. Next, tally the number of questions at each level. Count the total number of questions asked, and compute a percentage for each level.

Type of Question	Total Number of Questions
1. Memory: —What is another name for a living thing? —What are the characteristics common to all living things? —How do living things obtain food? —What kind of energy do plants need in order to carry out photosynthesis? —Who discovered the existence of microorganisms?	5
2. Translation: —Tell me in your own words what photosynthesis means. —Explain the meaning of spontaneous generation. —What is the derivation of metabolism?	3
3. Interpretation: —How does movement in plants differ from movement in animals? —What happens to energy taken into an organism?	2
4. Application: —What would happen to the plants in this room if they didn't get sun and water? —Diagram the concept of photosynthesis.	2
5. Analysis: —What are the similarities and differences between living and nonliving things? —Which of the scientist's experiments supported abiogenesis and which supported biogenesis? —How does the movement of an animal differ from the movement of a wind-up toy?	3

continued

Type of Question	Total Number of Questions
6. **Synthesis:** —Write a paper on pasteurization. Discuss what the process is, how it is done, and why it is done. —Do an oral report on how people do home canning from things that grow in their gardens. Explain how these procedures relate to the experiments on spontaneous generation described in this chapter.	2
7. **Evaluation:** —Whose experiments do you think were most effective: Spallanzani's, Needham's, or Pasteur's? Why?	1
TOTAL Number of Questions, All Levels:	18

Percentage of Memory <u>27%</u>; Translation <u>17%</u>; Interpretation <u>11%</u>; Application <u>11%</u>; Analysis <u>17%</u>; Synthesis <u>11%</u>; Evaluation <u>6%</u>

Checklists

A checklist is a simple structured tool to use while observing in a classroom. It serves the function of limiting the observation to the items on the list and allows the observer simply to mark when a task has been completed. The checklist does not evaluate; it documents.

Although many commercial checklists are available, the best are specifically designed for the observation at hand. As with all observational tools, it is essential that the observer limit the items on the checklist to the objectives set for the specific observation. The keys to developing a good checklist are: (1) knowing the purpose for the checklist and (2) developing items that help the observer determine whether the items looked for are found. Checklists can be designed to look for many things in the classroom, such as the classroom environment, classroom management techniques, elements of the curriculum, teaching styles, and competencies taught. We have provided one specific checklist for observing teaching styles. (Teaching styles are the unique ways that teachers organize instruction based on their philosophy of teaching and learning.)

SAMPLE FORM 8

Checklist for Determining Teaching Style

NAME OF OBSERVER: Jose Perez

DATE AND TIME OF OBSERVATION: October 17, 20—, 9:50 a.m.

TEACHER: Nisha Mendez

GRADE LEVEL AND/OR SUBJECT: Eighth grade; mathematics

OBJECTIVE OF OBSERVATION: To determine the teaching style of a particular teacher

Instructions to the Observer: Prior to the observation, read over the items below. These items represent various teaching styles used by teachers. During and after the observation, place an "x" next to those items you have observed.

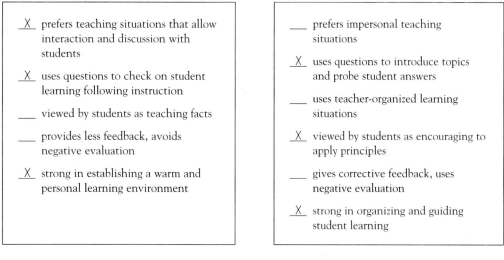

<u>X</u> prefers teaching situations that allow interaction and discussion with students

<u>X</u> uses questions to check on student learning following instruction

___ viewed by students as teaching facts

___ provides less feedback, avoids negative evaluation

<u>X</u> strong in establishing a warm and personal learning environment

___ prefers impersonal teaching situations

<u>X</u> uses questions to introduce topics and probe student answers

___ uses teacher-organized learning situations

<u>X</u> viewed by students as encouraging to apply principles

___ gives corrective feedback, uses negative evaluation

<u>X</u> strong in organizing and guiding student learning

Source: [online] Internet path: http://www.aismissstate.edu.\ALS/Unit9modulers.num and Dean Boyd, computer system coordinator, Mississippi State University of Starkville, MS, College of Agriculture and Life Sciences, September 22, 1999.

Structured Observation of a Lesson

One way to observe the structure of a lesson is to use a lesson-planning form on which elements of a lesson are outlined. The observer can watch a lesson being taught and outline the lesson using specific examples on the lesson-planning form. Of course, it is important to note that not all lessons have all the elements of a particular structure. And each element may be included in more than one lesson. Sometimes lessons include elements in a variety of orders. At times, only a few of the elements occur. We have chosen to provide an example based on the work of Madeline Hunter and developed by Lois Sprinthall. However, any lesson-planning form can be used.

SAMPLE FORM 9

Observation Form for Structured Observation of a Lesson

NAME OF OBSERVER: Angie Carl

DATE AND TIME OF OBSERVATION: November 11, 20—, 12:40 p.m.

TEACHER: Olivia Smith

GRADE LEVEL AND/OR SUBJECT: Seventh grade; social studies (Civil War)

OBJECTIVE OF OBSERVATION: To identify how the elements of a lesson are implemented by the teacher

continued

Instructions to the Observer: As you observe in the classroom, list the elements of the lesson under the categories below. A description of each category appears in italics.

1. **Anticipatory Set**—*In every lesson, the teacher provides initial motivation and focus for the lesson. Sometimes this focus takes the form of a review of previous knowledge important to this lesson; at other times it is designed to "grab" the students' attention. Key words: alerting, relevance, relationship (to previous lesson), meaningfulness, etc.*

   Teacher read from letters by two brothers, one fighting for the North, the other for the South. Students were attentive and appeared to be listening.

2. **Objective**—*In almost every lesson, the teacher specifies the behaviors the students will be expected to perform. In other words, the students know what is expected of them and what they are expected to learn.*

   Objective on board was pointed out to the students—"The student will compose a letter from the perspective of a soldier from the North or the South during the Civil War."

3. **Teacher Input**—*In most lessons, the teacher will provide the students with the information needed to reach the objective successfully. Sometimes, the teacher will show the students how to accomplish the task by modeling appropriate performance.*

   Using a variety of questioning techniques, the students and the teacher reviewed two battles discussed in previous lesson. Teacher listed key information on overhead projector.

   The students were reminded to be sure they had all this information in their notebooks since they will need it to complete their assignment.

4. **Checking for Understanding**—*Throughout the lesson, the teacher checks to ensure that the students understand the concepts or skills being taught. This can be accomplished through random questioning or individual tutoring.*

   The teacher asked the students if they understood the importance of the two battles. She then discussed with them how the perspective of the Northern and Southern soldiers would have differed in each battle.

   As the students worked together, the teacher circulated to be sure they were on task and understood what they were doing.

5. **Guided Practice**—*In every lesson, students practice the expected performance. This may include exercises completed with the teacher, examples done by students on the board, students reading aloud, students working together to complete assignments, games that allow the students to exhibit understanding, etc.*

   The teacher brainstormed with the students about a Southern soldier's impression of one of the two battles. The brainstorming was listed on the board—the information about the battle was still projected on the screen above the board.

   The teacher told the students to do the same in small groups from the perspective of a Northern soldier in the same battle.

   The teacher and the students composed on the overhead one letter from a Northern soldier to his sweetheart.

6. **Independent Practice**—*Student independently exhibit the behaviors set forth in the objective. To accomplish this, students might complete problems, write a paper, do an experiment, give a report, complete a project, do research, etc.*

   The students were instructed to begin a letter from either a Northern or Southern soldier to a member of his family or friend from the other battle. They were told to use the same process—first brainstorming by themselves about what that soldier was feeling, and then writing the letter.

7. **Closure**—*The teacher helps students review what they have learned in the lesson. This may include a summary of the lesson, questions about what happened during the students' independent practice, the students' report of their progress, an evaluation by the teacher, a discussion of the relationship of this lesson to the next lesson or the unit, or an assignment of additional independent practice.*

The teacher asked for a Northern and Southern volunteer to tell the class what he or she had written or brainstormed thus far.

Source: Lois Sprinthall, *A Strategy Guide for Teachers: Guide Book for Supervisors of Novice Teachers.* Unpublished manuscript. Based on the work of Madeline Hunter.

Interview Methods

Frequently, observations do not yield enough data for complete understanding of the situation. For example, it is not always possible to observe all the grouping patterns employed in a single classroom over a period of weeks. University students are unlikely to be able to return two weeks after an initial classroom observation to observe other classes of the same teacher. Therefore, observers are unable to see how the grouping patterns change and develop based on the students and the content. An interview with the teacher, when conducted objectively, can help the observer determine this sequence. The interview should be designed to reveal data that cannot be observed in one observation, or even in a series.

The interview is a fact-finding technique in which an attempt is made to obtain information from the respondent through direct questioning. Of course, a good interview requires planning and nonjudgmental questions that reveal important data.

Following is a checklist of important interview techniques to use prior to and during an interview.

SAMPLE FORM 10

Checklist of Interview Techniques

NAME OF OBSERVER: Maria Ortiz

DATE, TIME, AND PLACE OF OBSERVATION: November 6, 20—, 3:30 p.m., Teacher's classroom

PERSON TO BE INTERVIEWED: Mr. Maldonado

GRADE LEVEL AND/OR SUBJECT: Fifth grade

OBJECTIVE OF OBSERVATION: To find out about grouping patterns different from those observed on November 4, 20—

Instructions to the Observer: Review this checklist prior to and after your interview. Check off those items you have completed.

continued

1. Prior to the Interview

✓ Establish the purpose for the interview.

✓ Request an appointment (time and place), giving sufficient lead time for you and the person to be interviewed.

✓ Plan objective, specific questions related to the purpose of the interview.

✓ Prioritize questions, asking the most important first.

✓ Remind the person to be interviewed of the time, place, and purpose of the interview.

2. The Interview

✓ Arrive at the pre-established place several minutes before the scheduled time for the interview.

✓ Start the interview by reminding the person to be interviewed of its purpose.

✓ Request permission to tape the interview (if appropriate).

✓ If taping is unfeasible, take careful, objective notes, trying to list direct quotes as often as possible.

✓ Avoid inserting impressions or judgments.

✓ Limit the interview to no more than 15–30 minutes.

3. After the Interview

✓ Review with the respondent what has been said or heard.

✓ Express your appreciation for the interview.

✓ Offer to share the interview report with the respondent.

Observing Teaching Standards

Since the mid-1980s, professional teaching organizations have worked jointly to establish standards for what teachers should know (knowledge base) and be able to do (teaching competencies). One of these organizations, the Council of Chief State Officers, sponsored the formation of the Interstate New Teacher Assessment and Support Consortium (INTASC). INTASC has articulated a common core of teaching knowledge and skill that it contends should be acquired by all teachers. In this context, all teachers include preservice teachers, newly licensed teachers, and advanced certification teachers. The distinction between each teaching level is the degree of sophistication that teachers exhibit in application of knowledge rather than in the kind of knowledge needed to teach. For example, a preservice student teacher of high-school English should be fluent in English grammar and how to teach it. However, it may take several years of experience and, perhaps, even advanced degrees before a teacher is able to completely integrate the teaching of grammar with the teaching of writing.

Most states have adopted INTASC core standards to guide their teacher education and licensure reform efforts. Ten principles are included in the common core of standards. The rating scale on the next page allows preservice teachers to examine the level of sophistication attained by the teachers they observe. It should be noted that this scale would need to be utilized many times over a long period by sophisticated, advanced-certification teacher observers to provide an accurate picture of the teacher's level of sophistication in each of the core teaching standards. The rating scale appears in this text to assist preservice teachers in recognizing the common core teaching standards and learning how to assess their presence based on classroom performance. This rating scale is most useful as a self-evaluation instrument.

SAMPLE FORM 11

A Rating Scale for Observation of Standards for Teaching

NAME OF OBSERVER: Amy Anderson

DATE AND TIME OF OBSERVATION: May 16, 20—, 9:30 a.m.

LENGTH OF OBSERVATION: Approximately 45 minutes

TEACHER: Charles Doran

GRADE LEVEL OF OBSERVATION: Ninth grade

OBJECTIVE OF OBSERVATION: To examine the level of teaching standards exhibited by a particular teacher

Instructions to the Observer: Prior to your observation, read over each principle carefully. During and after your observation, put a check on the rating scale that best describes what you observed. The check may be either on or between the numbers 1–5. Note: This rating is based on one limited observation.

Content Pedagogy

Principle 1: The teacher understands the central concepts, tools of inquiry, and structures of the discipline(s) he or she teaches and can create learning experiences that make these aspects of subject matter meaningful to students.

1	2	3	4	✓ 5
Limited sophistication		Moderate sophistication		High sophistication

Student Development

Principle 2: The teacher understands how children learn and develop and can provide learning opportunities that support their intellectual, social, and personal development.

1	2	3	4	✓ 5
Limited sophistication		Moderate sophistication		High sophistication

Diverse Learners

Principle 3: The teacher understands how students differ in their approaches to learning and creates instructional opportunities that are adapted to diverse learners.

1	2	3 ✓	4	5
Limited sophistication		Moderate sophistication		High sophistication

continued

Multiple Instructional Strategies

Principle 4: The teacher understands and uses a variety of instructional strategies to encourage students' development of critical thinking, problem solving, and performance skills.

1	2	3	✓ 4	5
Limited sophistication		Moderate sophistication		High sophistication

Motivation and Management

Principle 5: The teacher uses an understanding of individual and group motivation and behavior to create a learning environment that encourages positive social interaction, active engagement in learning, and self-motivation.

1	2	3	4 ✓	5
Limited sophistication		Moderate sophistication		High sophistication

Communication and Technology

Principle 6: The teacher uses knowledge of effective verbal, nonverbal, and media communication techniques to foster active inquiry, collaboration, and supportive interaction in the classroom.

1	2	3	✓ 4	5
Limited sophistication		Moderate sophistication		High sophistication

Planning

Principle 7: The teacher plans instruction based on knowledge of subject matter, students, the community, and curriculum goals.

1	2	3	4 ✓	5
Limited sophistication		Moderate sophistication		High sophistication

Assessment

Principle 8: The teacher understands and uses formal and informal assessment strategies to evaluate and ensure the continuous intellectual, social, and physical development of the learner.

1	2	3	4	✓5
Limited sophistication		Moderate sophistication		High sophistication

Reflective Practice

Principle 9: The teacher is a reflective practitioner who continually evaluates the effects of his or her choices and actions on others (students, parents, and other professionals in the learning community) and who actively seeks out opportunities to grow professionally.

1	2	3	✓ 4	5
Limited sophistication		Moderate sophistication		High sophistication

School and Community Development

Principle 10: The teacher fosters relationships with school colleagues, parents, and agencies in the larger community to support students' learning and well-being.

1	2	3	4 ✓	5
Limited sophistication		Moderate sophistication		High sophistication

Source: Robert F. Yinger. "The Role of Standards in Teaching and Teacher Education" in *The Education of Teachers*. National Society for the Study of Education (NSSE), pp. 100–101, 1999.

SAMPLE FORM 12

Reflective Observation of Teachers

NAME OF OBSERVER: Angela Alexander

DATE AND TIME OF REFLECTIVE OBSERVATION: March 30, 20—, 12:45 p.m.

TEACHER: Raymond Davenport

GRADE LEVEL AND/OR SUBJECT: Eighth grade; mathematics

OBJECTIVE OF OBSERVATION: To think carefully and reflect about your observation of teachers. Below are some guiding questions/statements related to each of the five steps in the reflection cycle (Chapter One, p. 10). The questions/statements are directly related to the ten principles from the INTASC Standards (Chapter Two, pp. 37–39).

Instructions to the Observer: Use Form 12A to respond to the following questions after you have completed your observations of teachers

1. **Select**
   a. What two types of observation did you complete?
   b. What principles from INTASC standards did you address?

continued

2. **Describe**
    a. What grade level(s) did you observe?
    b. Briefly describe your anecdotal observations.
    c. Briefly describe your structured observations.
    d. Briefly describe the type of assessments you used.

3. **Analyze**
    a. How did your prior experience with observation of teachers influence this experience?
    b. How will your observation of different teaching styles affect your future teaching?

4. **Appraise**
    a. Describe the teacher-student interaction you observed. Was it appropriate?
    b. Did the ten principles based on the common core of standards (INTASC) influence your decision to become a teacher? Explain.

5. **Transform**
    a. What did you learn about teaching through your observation?
    b. What did you learn about types of assessment?
    c. How do you think this observation will help you in your future teaching?

Source: Adapted from North Carolina State Department of Public Instruction. *Performance Based Licensure*, Raleigh, NC, 1998–1999.

⑥ Chapter Three
Observing Classrooms, Schools, and Curriculum

Anecdotal Observation of Classrooms, Schools, and Curriculum

Anecdotal observations can be completed while observing the classroom, the school, and the curriculum. These observations can reveal many interesting aspects of the operation of the school and its instructional program and how individual teachers adapt the instructional program to their students. In addition, these observations can show how teachers and schools deal with physical constraints such as overcrowding, lack of equipment, and poor facilities.

Anecdotal Observations of Classrooms

An anecdotal observation of classroom organization includes a description of the physical environment and its layout. It is important to include information about the lighting source and whatever classroom decoration is displayed.

SAMPLE FORM 13

Form for Anecdotal Record of Classroom Organization

NAME OF OBSERVER: Marvin Anderson

DATE AND TIME OF OBSERVATION: September 19, 20—, 8:15 a.m.

LENGTH OF OBSERVATION: 30 minutes

PERSON AND/OR EVENT OBSERVED: Mr. Schroeder's classroom

GRADE LEVEL AND/OR SUBJECT: Fourth grade; all subjects

OBJECTIVE OF OBSERVATION: To see how Mr. Schroeder's classroom is organized

Instructions to the Observer: As completely and accurately as possible, describe the organization of the classroom. Be sure to include as much detail as possible. Try to avoid making judgments.

continued

The classroom is quite small for the 29 students. The students' desks are arranged in five rows of five or six desks each, with the chalkboard in the front. The desks have small cubbies in them and separate chairs. In the front of the room to the students' right is a stool and a small podium. To the students' left are windows that run the length of the room. The shades are pulled down against the morning sun. On the students' right are high windows that face the hallway; beneath these windows are bulletin boards. Mr. Schroeder's desk is at the rear of the classroom next to the exterior windows. Next to the window is a four-drawer file cabinet. On the other side of the teacher's desk is a student desk and chair. At the right rear is a student worktable and eight chairs. Behind the worktable, along most of the rear wall, are student cubbies and bookshelves. On the floor, there is a royal blue carpet that has many stains on it.

Light in the classroom is good. There is a lot of exterior light from outside and additional light from the hallway. The classroom is additionally lit by long fluorescent fixtures. Mr. Schroeder has a lamp on his desk, which is also lit. Under the exterior windows is a ledge. Under about one-quarter of the length of the ledge is the heating and cooling unit. The classroom is air-conditioned. Under the rest (of the ledge) there are bookcases and cabinets.

Above the front chalkboard is a bulletin board. On this board is a large poster with the classroom rules. Also on this bulletin board there are some mass-produced posters about the writing process and reading books. Near the center of this bulletin board, there is a group of a dozen or so hanging maps. On the bulletin boards to the students' right, there is an opening school display with all the students' photographs. Under each photo is a paper that each student wrote on the first day of school, introducing himself or herself to Mr. Schroeder. The next bulletin board is empty. Nearest the door to the hallway at the rear right are school announcements and the weekly list of classroom jobs. The jobs include plants, attendance, lunch monitor, hallway monitor, bus monitor, playground monitors, classroom monitors, and care of pets. The names of one or more students are listed next to each job. Along the top of the cubbies at the rear of the room there are plants. Next to the cubbies there is a watering can with a long spout. On top of one of the bookshelves there is an aquarium; nearby is a cage with two gerbils (I think).

Along the ledge, under the exterior windows, are what appear to be learning centers. Most seem to be related to the Revolutionary War. One deals with the battles of the revolution; another with the personalities of the war. I can't read the headings on the other two. Nearest the front of the room, on the ledge, there is a globe.

When the students enter the room it is very crowded. There is not much room between their desks, and they are continuously bumping into one another. It gets noisy very quickly. Mr. Schroeder is in the front of the room with the attendance monitor for the week, taking attendance and collecting lunch money. Several students are milling around the podium, trying to ask the teacher questions. Three boys are sitting at the table at the rear of the room. Mr. Schroeder walks up to them to tell them that they will have new desks by the end of the week, though he's not quite sure where they'll put them. The students on the left side of the room are so close to the ledge that it would not be possible to use the learning centers without moving their desks. (I'll watch to see how Mr. Schroeder handles this later.) A girl raises her hand and asks if she can go to the restroom to get water for the gerbils. Mr. Schroeder says, "Take the restroom pass and the watering can, and also get enough water for the plants." She leaves.

The intercom clicks on and Mr. Schroeder attempts to "shush" the talking students. They get quieter but continue to talk. He walks to the rear of the room and flicks the lights; most of the students quiet down. However, the boys at the rear table are still talking. He walks over to them, and points to the classroom rules, one of which is "Respect others when they are speaking." They quiet down.

When the announcements are over, Mr. Schroeder has each of the three boys go to a chart under the class rules and put a check next to his name. If the students get five checks during the week, they cannot participate in Fun Friday, which is an event that occurs each Friday afternoon.

Another method of classroom observation is to draw a simple diagram of the classroom, illustrating the seating arrangement and the placement of furniture and equipment. Since a diagram cannot show what is on the bulletin boards or walls, the observer should discuss these elements after mapping the classroom.

SAMPLE FORM 14

Form for a Classroom Map

NAME OF OBSERVER: Kim Philbeck

DATE AND TIME OF OBSERVATION: September 16, 20—, 9:15 a.m.

PERSON AND/OR EVENT OBSERVED: Mrs. Romano

GRADE LEVEL AND/OR SUBJECT: Eleventh-grade; American history

OBJECTIVE OF OBSERVATION: To determine how the organization of the classroom relates to instruction, management, and motivation of students

Instructions to the Observer: First, draw a map of the classroom you are observing, including seating arrangements, placement of furniture, computers, telephone, and other equipment. Then, give a brief anecdotal description of these classroom elements: use of technology, lighting, traffic patterns, instructional displays, management, and motivational elements.

1. Draw classroom map:

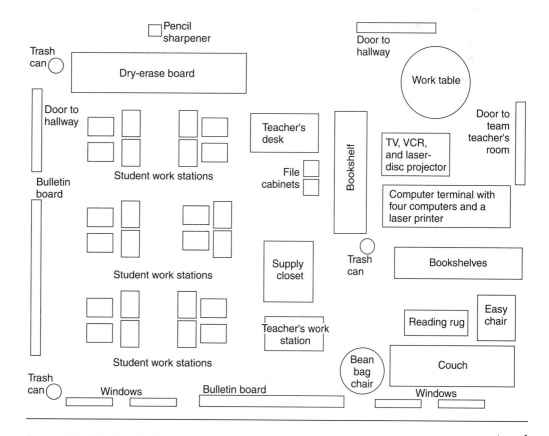

Courtesy of Kim Philbeck and Stephanie Price, Preservice teachers, UNC Ashville.

continued

2. Anecdotal description of classroom elements:

The students' desks are arranged in clusters because group work is one of the main instructional strategies used by Mrs. Romano. However, the students also have enough space in between the desks to work independently. Some of the students have to twist their heads around or move their seats to be facing the dry-erase board and the main instructional area of the classroom. Mrs. Romano is very flexible, however, and allows students to move their desks to face the front of the room during instructional time. When the time comes to work in small groups, the students move their desks back into clusters. The clusters of desks are spread out so the teacher can easily move around the room to reach each student. A reading corner with comfortable seating and many books is in the corner of the classroom. Supplies are centrally located with plenty of floor space surrounding the supply closet and the teacher's workstation (where homework and assignments are turned in), since those are high-traffic areas.

(a) Use of Technology:
The classroom contains four computer terminals and is equipped with a laser printer. Students are assigned computer time each week to draft papers (students are learning how to use desktop publishing to publish their work) or use other educational software. A TV, VCR, and laserdisc projector are located on a rolling cart beside the computer terminals. The cart can be rolled to the main instructional area when the equipment is used in presentations. Mrs. Romano's computer is facing away from students' desks to deter wandering eyes. The file cabinet is located in the corner behind her desk and is not accessible to the students.

(b) Lighting and Traffic Patterns:
The students' desks are facing the board rather than facing the door or windows. This is to prevent students' preoccupation with events outside of the classroom. It also makes it easier for them to see the board since the light is not in their eyes. The desks are in an inverted-V formation. In the corner of the room, Mrs. Romano has a designated private area. The computer terminals are separated from the student workstations and the reading corner by bookcases, which ensures as little disruption as possible for students in all spaces in the classroom. The overhead projector is permanently located so it remains safe and does not block the students' view of the board. The V formation allows easy movement through the aisles and accessible monitoring of students by Mrs. Romano. Students can also enter and exit by either the side or center aisles.

(c) Instructional Displays, Management, and Motivational Elements:
There are two long bulletin boards. The side bulletin board contains things pertinent to what is to be covered. There are numerous displays on the bulletin boards across the wall and opposite the window wall. Rules and consequences are posted on the front wall so students will be reminded of them daily. Resources are located in the back of the room and out of students' way until they are needed. There is also a table in the back corner for peer tutoring. There are computers in the room for students to use if they finish early with classwork. Mrs. Romano models procedures on one of the classroom computers; then students can go to the library or computer lab to carry out individual work. Classroom computers are used only for word processing and Internet research. Students must sign up to use computers. Their usage is limited to 30 minutes. Parents have to sign a form before students can use the Internet.

Many other anecdotal observations of the classroom can be useful. For example, observers may focus on the instructional elements of the classroom or on how the students move throughout the classroom for certain purposes. Marvin notes in his anecdotal discussion of Mr. Schroeder's classroom that it is crowded, and that three of the students do not yet have their own desks. Marvin may want to spend part of a day observing how Mr. Schroeder deals with this problem. If the students are using the learning centers during social studies, what happens to the student desks nearest the ledge? Does Mr. Schroeder use the rear table for reading or other groups? What happens to the three boys if they are not a part of the group using the table? When students leave the classroom for special classes, how do they do so without disturbing the other students?

Anecdotal Observations of Schools

Similar anecdotal observations can be done on various aspects of an entire school. Observing students in hallways during a change of class periods can reveal a great deal about the organization of the school. It is also interesting to examine the "decorations" in the hallways. Are there bulletin boards displaying student work? Do the bulletin boards have locked glass doors? Are there display cabinets in the hallways? What is in these cabinets? Are the hallways well lit? Do the students have individual lockers? Where are the various school administrative offices? Are they easily accessible to students, teachers, and visitors? How are the offices furnished? What are the "decorations" in the offices, such as the guidance office, that caters to students? What are the school's grounds like? How about the lunchroom, auditorium, and gym? Are there public areas in which students gather? Where are they, and what are they like? What is the playground like? Is there playground equipment? Examining all of these elements helps the observer become more familiar with the school.

Anecdotal Observations of Curriculum

Anecdotal observations can also be used to examine the curriculum. The observer in Mr. Schroeder's classroom might want to know more about the social studies curriculum. He might write an anecdotal observation that includes information about the text and other classroom materials. Or, he might discuss more detailed information about the learning centers. The observer might seek out the school, district, or state curriculum guide to see what is taught in fourth-grade social studies. How does what Mr. Schroeder is teaching relate to what is required by the school, district, or state? The observer might compare Mr. Schroeder's interpretation of the curriculum in his lessons with the interpretation of another fourth-grade teacher. All of these elements can tell the observer a great deal about the school, its curriculum, and its instructional policies.

Structured Observation of Classrooms, Schools, and Curriculum

Structured observations of classrooms, schools, and curriculum can be conducted by using the techniques of coding, checklists, interviews, and surveys. Structured observations allow the observer to look for very specific elements. Instruments may be developed by the observer, adapted from other sources, or copied from this text.

Observing the Social Environment in a Classroom

There are numerous ways to look at the social environment in a classroom. We will discuss one way that is based on the research of Talcott Parsons and Edward A. Shills (1951) and Herbert J. Walberg and Gary J. Anderson (1968). Their research has led to the development of fifteen dimensions of a classroom social environment. Those dimensions, with brief descriptions developed by Gary D. Borich (1990), are as follows:

1. **Cohesiveness**—When a group of individuals interacts for a period of time, a feeling of intimacy or togetherness develops. Too much cohesiveness within a classroom may separate members of the group from nonmembers, and reduce the motivation and willingness of some students to become engaged in the learning process. Too little cohesiveness may discourage students from an allegiance to group norms and encourage them to focus exclusively on their own personal interests and desires.

2. **Diversity**—The extent to which the class provides for different student interests and activities is important to school learning. Too much diversity in a classroom can make teaching to the average student difficult, while too little may fail to respond to individual learning needs.

3. **Formality**—The extent to which behavior within a class is guided by formal rules can influence the flexibility both teacher and students may need to achieve stated goals. A classroom with an extensive or inflexible system of rules and procedures may be less productive than a classroom with fewer rules that are phased in and out or changed periodically to accommodate changing goals and conditions.

4. **Speed**—Student commitment to the goals of the class is best achieved when students feel they are learning at the same rate as other students. Too fast a pace will discourage a commitment to group goals for less able learners, while too slow a pace will discourage a commitment from more able learners.

5. **Environment**—The classroom physical environment, including the amount of space and type of equipment, can influence the structure of the group and relationships among its members. Generally the more the classroom reflects the world outside, the more opportunity there is to learn from its environment.

6. **Friction**—This refers to the extent to which certain students are responsible for class tension and hostility among members of the class. The greater the friction, the more time spent on classroom management, leaving the students less task-oriented.

7. **Goal direction**—Clearly stated goals and their acceptance by the group orient the class and provide expected roles for class members. Students in highly goal-directed classes are expected to reach instructional goals more quickly than those in classes where the goals are unspecified.

8. **Favoritism**—This indicates the extent to which some students and the teacher behave in ways that benefit some at the expense of others. A classroom in which there are many "favorites" lessens the self-concepts of those who are not and disengages them from a commitment to class goals.

9. **Cliquishness**—Cliques within a class can lead to hostility among class members and alternate norms, causing less optimal group productivity. A high degree of cliquishness can distract and cause them to move off-task, especially during group work when students may be loyal to the clique and not obedient to the teacher.

10. **Satisfaction**—Student's learning abilities are affected when they gain a sense of accomplishment from completing the events and activities that are assigned. Low satisfaction

or low sense of accomplishment leads to greater frustration and less interest in the class, eventually reducing a student's need to achieve.

11. **Disorganization**—Class disorganization is believed to be related to reduced instructional time and, therefore, reduced opportunity to learn. Extreme disorganization can result in classroom management problems and large increases in the time needed to achieve instructional goals.

12. **Difficulty**—Generally, students who perceive the content as easy tend to perform more poorly on measures of achievement than those who do not. A high degree of perceived difficulty, however, will make some students give up and disengage from the learning task.

13. **Apathy**—Students who fail to see the purpose or relevance of class activities to themselves perform more poorly than those who do. Those students fail to behave according to the accepted group norms, which increases both the rate of misbehavior and the time spent on classroom management.

14. **Democratic**—This indicates where the class perceives itself on the authoritarian-democratic continuum. Optimal learning may occur under both extremes, depending on the degree of warmth perceived by students. An authoritarian climate in which the teacher is warm and nurturing may be as productive for learning as a democratic climate in which students have greater control over their learning environment.

15. **Competitiveness**—The effect of competitiveness has been shown to differ widely both within and across classrooms. Too little or too much competitiveness is believed to be detrimental to learning, with repetitive cycles of competition and cooperation being optimal.

Based on these dimensions, Borich developed a coding scale on which the observer indicates the level to which three elements of each dimension are observed in the classroom. An average score for each dimension on this scale, particularly when it is employed several times in the same classroom, can help observers become aware of various elements of a classroom's social environment. Borich points out that the scale is not appropriate for research purposes, but is particularly useful if observers complete several administrations of it while observing a variety of grouping patterns, across subject areas, over a long period of time.

SAMPLE FORM 15

Form for Coding Scale of Classroom Social Environment

NAME OF OBSERVER: Enrique Valdez

DATE AND TIME OF OBSERVATION: January 15, 20—, 10:40 a.m.

LENGTH OF OBSERVATION: 50 minutes

PERSON AND/OR EVENT OBSERVED: Sara Schmidtson's classroom

GRADE LEVEL AND/OR SUBJECT: First grade; mathematics

OBJECTIVE OF OBSERVATION: To observe the classroom social environment

continued

Instructions to the Observer: Before using the coding scale, become familiar with each of the fifteen dimensions that describe the classroom social environment on pages 46, 47.

Each dimension is divided into three elements (or statements). Each of these three elements appears in the same order, once per set, in the three sets that comprise the coding scale.

To use the coding scale effectively, you should circle the appropriate rating and average the scores *for all three statements* in any given dimension(s) you want to examine. For example, to study classroom diversity, you would compare the scores for numbers 2, 17, and 32.

The scale may also be used to determine what you might want to examine further. Thus, after one or more classroom observations, you may want to average the scores for all three sets, and then pick out those that stand out in some way.

When scoring, you should note the following: (1) some statements are phrased negatively and, thus, their ratings have been reversed, and (2) in several of the dimensions being measured (diversity, speed, difficulty, democracy, and competitiveness), a higher score is not necessarily more desirable.

Dimension Elements	Strongly Disagree	Disagree	Strongly Agree	Agree	No Information
Set 1					
1. A student in this class has the chance to get to know all other students (cohesiveness).	1	2	3	④	N/I
2. The class has students with many different interests (diversity).	1	2	3	④	N/I
3. There is a set of rules for the students to follow (formality).	1	2	3	④	N/I
4. Most of the class has difficulty keeping up with the assigned work (speed).	1	②	3	4	N/I
5. The books and equipment students need or want are easily available in the classroom (environment).	1	2	3	④	N/I
6. There are tensions among certain students that tend to interfere with class activities (friction).	1	②	3	4	N/I
7. Most students have little idea of what the class is attempting to accomplish (goal direction).	④	3	2	1	N/I
8. The better students' questions are answered more sympathetically than those of the average students (favoritism).	1	2	③	4	N/I
9. Some students refuse to mix with the rest of the class (cliquishness).	1	2	③	4	N/I
10. The students seem to enjoy their classwork (satisfaction).	1	2	③	4	N/I
11. There are long periods during which the class does nothing (disorganization).	①	2	3	4	N/I
12. Some students in the class consider the work difficult (difficulty).	1	2	③	4	N/I
13. Most students seem to have a concern for the progress of the class (apathy).	4	③	2	1	N/I
14. When group discussions occur, all students tend to contribute (democracy).	1	②	3	4	N/I
15. Most students cooperate rather than compete with one another in this class (competitiveness).	4	3	②	1	N/I

Dimension Elements	Strongly Disagree	Disagree	Strongly Agree	Agree	No Information
Set 2					
16. Students in this class are not in close enough contact to develop likes and dislikes for one another (cohesiveness).	4	③	2	1	N/I
17. The class is working toward many different goals (diversity).	1	②	3	4	N/I
18. Students who break the rules are penalized (formality).	1	2	3	④	N/I
19. The class has plenty of time to cover the prescribed amount of work (speed).	4	3	②	1	N/I
20. A comprehensive collection of reference material is available in the classroom for students to use (environment).	1	②	3	4	N/I
21. Certain students seem to have no respect for other students (friction).	1	2	③	4	N/I
22. The objectives of the class are not clearly recognized (goal direction).	④	3	2	1	N/I
23. Every member of the class is given the same privileges (favoritism).	4	3	②	1	N/I
24. Certain students work only with their close friends (cliquishness).	1	2	③	4	N/I
25. There is considerable student dissatisfaction with the classwork (satisfaction).	④	3	2	1	N/I
26. Classwork is frequently interrupted by some students with nothing to do (disorganization).	4	③	2	1	N/I
27. Most students in this class are constantly challenged (difficulty).	1	②	3	4	N/I
28. Some members of the class don't care what the class does (apathy).	1	2	③	4	N/I
29. Certain students have more influence on the class than others (democracy).	4	3	2	①	N/I
30. Most students in the class want their work to be better than their friends' work (competitiveness).	1	2	③	4	N/I
Set 3					
31. This class is made up of individuals who do not know each other well (cohesiveness).	4	③	2	1	N/I
32. Different students are interested in different aspects of the class (diversity).	4	3	②	1	N/I
33. There is a right and wrong way of going about class activities (formality).	④	3	2	1	N/I
34. There is little time in this class for daydreaming (speed).	4	3	②	1	N/I
35. There are bulletin board displays and pictures around the room (environment).	4	3	2	①	N/I
36. Certain students in this class are uncooperative (friction).	1	2	3	④	N/I
37. Most of the class realizes exactly how much work is required (goal direction).	1	2	3	④	N/I
38. Certain students in the class are favored over others (favoritism).	①	2	3	4	N/I

continued

Dimension Elements	Strongly Disagree	Disagree	Strongly Agree	Agree	No Information
39. Most students cooperate equally well with all class members (cliquishness).	4	3	2	(1)	N/I
40. After an assignment, most students have a sense of satisfaction (satisfaction).	1	2	3	(4)	N/I
41. The class is well-organized and efficient (disorganization).	4	3	2	(1)	N/I
42. Most students consider the subject matter easy (difficulty).	4	3	(2)	1	N/I
43. Students show a common concern for the success of the class (apathy).	4	3	2	(1)	N/I
44. Each member of the class has as much influence as does any other member (democracy).	4	3	2	(1)	N/I
45. Students compete to see who can do the best work (competitiveness).	(4)	3	2	1	N/I

Source: Gary Borich. *Observation Skills for Effective Teaching,* pp. 113–115, 1990.

Student Assessments Used in the Classroom

Because students learn in different ways, it is important that teachers develop diverse techniques for assessing student skills and progress. Below is a checklist to help student observers indicate the evaluation tools used in the classroom to assess student work.

SAMPLE FORM 16

Checklist to Determine Student Assessments in the Classroom

NAME OF OBSERVER: Loyda Chacon

DATE AND TIME OF OBSERVATION: December 12, 20—, 8:45 a.m.

PERSON AND/OR EVENT OBSERVED: Mr. Ramos

GRADE LEVEL AND/OR SUBJECT: Fourth grade

SCHOOL: Riverside Elementary

OBJECTIVE OF OBSERVATION: To determine various assessment techniques

Instructions to the Observer: After structured observation or an interview with the classroom teacher, put a check in the appropriate column. List additional assessments where required next to items marked with an asterisk.

Type of Assessment	Observed	From Interview
1. Commercial Workbooks in Curricular Areas 　Reading 　Mathematics 　Science 　Social Studies 　Language Arts 　Others* (*handwriting*)	/ / / /	
2. Duplicated Sheets	/	/
3. Homework Assignments		/
4. Oral Presentation/Report		/
5. Hands-On Performance 　Computers 　Science Experiment 　Construction Project 　Dramatic Performances/Skits 　Chalkboard Work 　Art Project 　Musical Production 　Classroom Displays/Bulletin Board 　School Displays 　Others*	/ / / / / / /	/ / /
6. Written Work 　Reports 　Research Projects 　Creative Writing 　Others*	/ /	/
7. Teacher-Made Tests		/
8. Prepared Tests From Students' Texts		/
9. Standardized Tests		/
10. State Competency Tests		/
11. State End-of-Year Tests	/	
12. Anecdotal Records 　Writing Journals/Folders 　Art Folders 　Cumulative Record Folders 　Portfolios 　Others*	/ /	/ /
13. Others*		

Examining the Teaching of Required Material

Most schools have a guide describing the required curriculum for each subject and the skills or competencies that the students are expected to learn. The guide may be produced at the school or school-district level and is usually based on state requirements. A checklist for examining which competency is actually performed in the classroom can be designed based on the objectives or content outline of any curriculum guide. For example, if you are observing in an eleventh-grade history class as in the sample below, you can design a checklist based on what the students are required to learn in history, according to the curriculum guide. As you observe, you can check off those activities that are actually performed. Sample

Form 17, a checklist based on 1998 goals and performance indicators set by the North Carolina State Department of Public Instruction for eleventh-grade history, is partially listed below and is not filled in because the method is relatively simple, and each state will have its own curricular requirements. Form 17A can be found at the end of the book on page 00. You should design your own checklist based on the curricular requirements in the school in which you are observing.

SAMPLE FORM 17

Checklist of Goals, Objectives, and Competencies Covered in an Eleventh-Grade History Classroom

NAME OF OBSERVER: Julie Lo

DATE AND TIME OF OBSERVATION: October 14, 20—, 11:00 a.m.

TEACHER: Mr. Siskell

SCHOOL: Freedom High School

OBJECTIVE OF OBSERVATION: To acquaint the student with curriculum guide, then list goals and performance indicator for a subject being taught in the school observed.

Instructions to the Observer: Use the list of goals and performance indicators from a curriculum guide to develop your own checklist. For an example of a checklist of goals and performance indicators in an eleventh-grade history classroom, see below. If the competency, goal, objective and/or performance indicator is observed, place an "X" in the right-hand column.

Goals	Performance Indicators	Observed
1. The learner will analyze those elements in the American colonial experience that led to separation from England.	1.1 Describe how geographic diversity influenced economic, social, and political life in colonial North America.	X
	1.2 Describe the contributions of various racial, ethnic, and religious groups, including African Americans and Native Americans, to the development of a new culture.	X
	1.3 Elaborate on the sources of American nationalism.	
	1.4 Distinguish between immediate and long-term causes of the American Revolution.	X
	1.5 Assess the importance of military engagements, personalities, and geopolitical factors in the defeat of the British.	X
2. The learner will apply ideas of self-government as expressed in America's founding documents.	2.1 Trace the development of concepts of self-government in British North America from the Mayflower Compact to the Declaration of Independence.	

Goals	Performance Indicators	Observed
	2.2 Associate ideas in the founding documents with their European origins.	
	2.3 Analyze the Declaration of Independence and the Constitution of the United States as expressions of self-government.	X
	2.4 Evaluate the arguments of *The Federalist Papers* and the *Anti-Federalist Papers* as expressions of differing theories about self-government.	X
	2.5 Judge the extent to which the Bill of Rights extended the Constitution.	X
3. The learner will judge the effectiveness of the institutions of the new nation in completing its independence (1781–1815).	3.1 Identify major domestic problems of the nation under the Articles of Confederation and judge the extent to which they were resolved by the new Constitution.	X
	3.2 Judge the extent to which the institutions of the new nation protected the liberties of all its inhabitants.	
	3.3 Trace the development of religious liberty and tolerance in the new nation.	X
	3.4 Analyze the effects of territorial expansion and the admission of new states to the union.	
	3.5 Assess commercial and diplomatic relationships with Britain, France, and other nations.	X
	3.6 Evaluate the extent to which the United States was a "nation at risk" until 1815.	
4. The learner will assess the contending forces of nationalism and sectionalism in the period 1815–1850.	4.1 Map westward expansion and make inferences about its importance to African Americans and Native Americans.	X
	4.2 Analyze economic developments and judge their effects on nationalism and sectionalism.	
	4.3 Assess political events and personalities in terms of their influence on nationalistic or sectional trends.	X
	4.4 Analyze literary and artistic movements of the period as contributors to nationalism and sectionalism.	
	4.5 Evaluate the role of religion in the debate over slavery and in other social movements and changes of the period.	X
5. The learner will evaluate the Civil War and Reconstruction as affirmations of the power of the national government.	5.1 Elaborate on economic, social, and political conditions in the decade preceding the Civil War.	X
	5.2 Analyze long-term and immediate causes of the war and assess the extent to which slavery was the cause of the conflict.	X
	5.3 Trace important military and political events of the war period, and judge their significance to the outcome of the conflict.	X
	5.4 Judge immediate and long-term effects of Reconstruction on the daily lives of people as well as on the politics and economy of the former Confederate states.	X

Source: Adapted from North Carolina State Department of Public Instruction. *Social Studies Curriculum.* Raleigh, NC, 1998.

Examining Curriculum Strategies that Address Multiple Intelligences

You have probably already studied Howard Gardner's theory of multiple intelligences (1993). According to Gardner, the following seven intelligences are not fixed or static, can be taught and learned, and are multi-dimensional, occurring at multiple levels in the brain and body. Gardner's studies at Harvard University identified the following types of intelligence:

1. **Verbal/Linguistic**—The use of words.
2. **Logical/Mathematical**—The use of numbers and reasoning strategies.
3. **Spatial**—Involving pictures and images.
4. **Bodily**—Using the hands and body.
5. **Musical**—The use of tones, rhymes, and rhythms.
6. **Interpersonal**—Social understanding.
7. **Intrapersonal**—Self-knowledge.

Sample Form 18 is a checklist for each intelligence of possible teaching strategies that can be utilized and observed in the classroom. Sample Form 18A (page 161) is the form you will use as you observe teaching, the classroom environment, and learning.

SAMPLE FORM 18

Examination of Curricular Strategies That Challenge Students' Multiple Intelligences

NAME OF OBSERVER: Oscar Miller

DATE AND TIME OF OBSERVATION: February 18, 20—, 9:00 a.m.

TEACHER: Mrs. Hewitt

SCHOOL: Hayden Elementary School

OBJECTIVE OF OBSERVATION: To observe curricular strategies that challenge students' multiple intelligences

Instructions to the Observer: A list of curricular descriptors that challenge students' multiple intelligences is given below. Place a check before each descriptor observed.

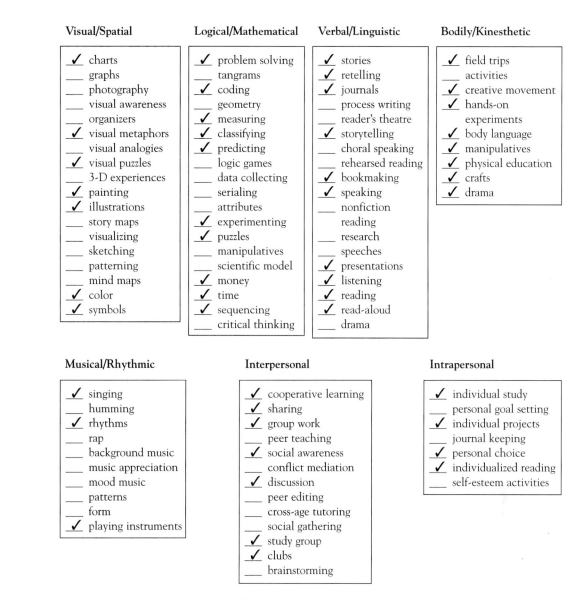

Visual/Spatial

- ✓ charts
- ___ graphs
- ___ photography
- ___ visual awareness
- ___ organizers
- ✓ visual metaphors
- ___ visual analogies
- ✓ visual puzzles
- ___ 3-D experiences
- ✓ painting
- ✓ illustrations
- ___ story maps
- ___ visualizing
- ___ sketching
- ___ patterning
- ___ mind maps
- ✓ color
- ✓ symbols

Logical/Mathematical

- ✓ problem solving
- ___ tangrams
- ✓ coding
- ___ geometry
- ✓ measuring
- ✓ classifying
- ✓ predicting
- ___ logic games
- ___ data collecting
- ___ serialing
- ___ attributes
- ✓ experimenting
- ✓ puzzles
- ___ manipulatives
- ___ scientific model
- ✓ money
- ✓ time
- ✓ sequencing
- ___ critical thinking

Verbal/Linguistic

- ✓ stories
- ✓ retelling
- ✓ journals
- ___ process writing
- ___ reader's theatre
- ✓ storytelling
- ___ choral speaking
- ___ rehearsed reading
- ✓ bookmaking
- ✓ speaking
- ___ nonfiction reading
- ___ research
- ___ speeches
- ✓ presentations
- ✓ listening
- ✓ reading
- ✓ read-aloud
- ___ drama

Bodily/Kinesthetic

- ✓ field trips
- ___ activities
- ✓ creative movement
- ✓ hands-on experiments
- ✓ body language
- ✓ manipulatives
- ✓ physical education
- ✓ crafts
- ✓ drama

Musical/Rhythmic

- ✓ singing
- ___ humming
- ✓ rhythms
- ___ rap
- ___ background music
- ___ music appreciation
- ___ mood music
- ___ patterns
- ___ form
- ✓ playing instruments

Interpersonal

- ✓ cooperative learning
- ✓ sharing
- ✓ group work
- ___ peer teaching
- ✓ social awareness
- ___ conflict mediation
- ✓ discussion
- ___ peer editing
- ___ cross-age tutoring
- ___ social gathering
- ✓ study group
- ✓ clubs
- ___ brainstorming

Intrapersonal

- ✓ individual study
- ___ personal goal setting
- ✓ individual projects
- ___ journal keeping
- ✓ personal choice
- ✓ individualized reading
- ___ self-esteem activities

Source: Adapted from the Simcoe District School Board. Midhurst, Ontario, Canada, 1996. [on-line] Internet path: http://www.scdsb.on.ca/

Examination of a Curriculum Guide

Examining the curriculum guide of the school, district, or state for the grade level and/or subject area you are observing can help you better understand the materials that are used in the classroom and the methods of instruction that are employed.

SAMPLE FORM 19

Form for Examining a Curriculum Guide

NAME OF EXAMINER: Sam Ruloff

DATE AND TIME OF EXAMINATION: November 22, 20—, 2:00 p.m.

OBJECTIVE OF EXAMINATION: To examine a curriculum guide and relate it to classroom curriculum

Instructions to the Examiner: Select a curriculum guide for the grade level and/or subject you will be observing. Complete this short answer survey.

1. Title of the guide: <u>The Visual Arts Curriculum Guide</u>

2. Check one: The guide is from the school ___ ; the school district <u>✓</u> ; the state ___ ; other (specify) _____

3. Date of the guide: <u>1985</u>

4. Grade level(s) of the guide: <u>(7–9)—(10–12)</u>

5. Subject area(s) of the guide: <u>Art-Painting, Printing, Graphics, Ceramics, Jewelry, Sculpture, Commercial Design, Weaving</u>

Answer the following yes/no or as indicated:

6. The guide includes: objectives <u>Yes</u>, student activities <u>Yes</u>, resources <u>Yes</u>, examples <u>Yes</u>, bibliographies <u>Yes</u>, computer software sources <u>No</u>, test banks <u>No</u>, discussion questions <u>No</u>, material for making transparencies <u>No</u>, content outlines <u>No</u>, other (specify) <u>Procedures—Slides, Films, Visiting Artists</u>

7. The guide suggests appropriate textbooks (specify): <u>Drawing with Ink, Creative Embroidery, The Picture History of Painting</u>

8. The guide suggests appropriate supplemental books. <u>Yes</u>

9. The guide suggests appropriate references. <u>Yes</u>

10. The guide suggests activities for different levels of students (i.e., gifted, advanced, basic, etc.) <u>Provides choices, in some areas. Suggestions for advanced/gifted.</u>

Examining Multicultural/Antibias Education in the Classroom

Examining multicultural/antibias education reflects a commitment to diversity and equity in the classroom. As you observe in your classroom, look for this commitment.

SAMPLE FORM 20

Checklist for a Multicultural/Antibias Education Evaluation

NAME OF OBSERVER: Loyola Hanks

DATE AND TIME OF OBSERVATION: March 6, 20—, 10:30 a.m.

SCHOOL: South Central Middle School

GRADE LEVELS OF SCHOOL: Fourth through seventh

OBJECTIVE OF OBSERVATION: To examine multicultural/antibias education in the classroom

Instructions to the Observer: After examining the school's curriculum (using Forms 17 and 19) and observing in numerous classrooms, complete the following evaluation checklist. Place a checkmark below the word or phrase that best describes your observations. Respond only to those items that were observable by you. Use Form 20A for the classroom in which you are observing.

	Not at all	Some	Large Amount
1. The classroom environment is reflective of diversity.			✓
2. Curriculum focuses on discrete pieces about cultures of various racial and ethnic groups.			✓
3. Multicultural activities are added on to the "regular" curriculum (i.e., celebrating various holidays of other cultures).			✓
4. Families or caregivers are asked to provide information about the most visible aspects of their cultural heritage (i.e., food, music, and holidays).			
5. Languages of children (other than English) are used in songs or other communication.			✓
6. The curriculum explores cultural differences among the children's families.		✓	
7. Staff members actively incorporate their children's daily life experiences into daily curriculum.		✓	
8. Curriculum and teacher-child interactions meet the cultural as well as individual developmental needs of their children.			✓
9. Parents' or family caregivers' knowledge about their native cultural background is utilized.			
10. Staff members intentionally encourage the children's development of critical thinking and tools for resisting prejudice and biased behaviors directed at themselves or others.		✓	
11. Staff members reflect the cultural and language diversity of the children and families they serve.			✓

Source: Adapted from Louise Derman-Sparks. *Young Children.* 54(5) 43. Pacific Oaks College, Pasadena, CA.

A Survey of Media

Since so many teachers use films, videos, cassettes, filmstrips, Powerpoint presentations and other media in their classrooms, it is helpful for student observers to learn a methodology for examining them. Below, are some forms that you can use to examine and evaluate some of the media used in the classroom.

SAMPLE FORM 21

Form for Technology Usage in the Classroom or Lab

NAME OF OBSERVER: Martha Henderson

DATE AND TIME OF OBSERVATION: May 15, 20—, 11:45 a.m.

SCHOOL: Westside Elementary School

TEACHER: Doris Kemp

GRADE LEVEL AND/OR SUBJECT: Fourth Grade; social studies

OBJECTIVE OF OBSERVATION: To observe how the available technology in the classroom or lab is used with students

Instructions to the Observer: It is important to determine whether technology is used to augment instruction in subject areas for the students or whether it is used to teach students technological skills and/or how to use particular applications. Answer the following questions to help identify how technology is being used in the class you are observing.

1. What is the objective(s) of the lesson being observed?
   To increase children's interest in reading books that support the social studies curriculum.

2. Does the use of technology match or reflect the learning objectives for the lesson?
   Yes.

3. How does the use of technology enhance the opportunity for students to meet the lesson's objectives?
   The software program allows students to explore over seventy-five novels, biographies, and other texts that support the social studies curriculum in American history.

4. Is technology used as a teaching tool by the teacher to present concepts and information in a particular subject area?
   Yes.

5. Is technology used to teach computer skills? If so, what skills?
   No.

6. Is the teacher's role during the lesson to guide students as they use technology or is his/her role to present information/skills?
   The teacher presented the database of books for use in social studies.

7. Is the use of the technology appropriate for the age and skill of the students?
   Yes.

8. Is equitable time provided for all students to use technology?
   Yes.

9. When technology is used, are students engaged in cooperative learning?
   No.

10. Is technology introduced for independent use, small-group use, or whole-class use?
   Independent or small-group work.

11. Does the lesson using technology provide an opportunity for student evaluation or feedback? If so, describe the opportunity. If not, ask the teacher why not.
   No. The teacher will ask for feedback at the end of the social studies unit.

Source: Jean Camp, Instructional Technology Coordinator, The University of North Carolina at Greensboro. Unpublished. Courtesy of Mary Olson, The University of North Carolina at Greensboro.

A Survey of Computer Software

As computer software has become more readily available at affordable prices, it is increasingly important that teachers assess and evaluate the software not only in terms of its content, but also in terms of its appropriateness to the curriculum and the age and ability of the students. Likewise, student teachers should examine the software to determine if its maturity level and accuracy warrant its use with individuals, small-groups, or the entire class. Sample Form 22 is a simple guide for examining computer software.

SAMPLE FORM 22

Software Evaluation Form

NAME OF EXAMINER: Jean Smith

DATE AND TIME OF EXAMINATION: March 17, 20—, 10:45 a.m.

SOFTWARE TITLE: Sounds and Letters

PUBLISHER: Software Support Publishing Company

PUBLICATION DATE: 1996

OBJECTIVE OF OBSERVATION: To increase students' knowledge of programs that focus on the Alphabetic Principle and Phonemic Awareness

Instructions to the Examiner: Determine the parameters of the software package by checking the appropriate blank. Answer the questions related to rating the software. Then rate the product on a scale of 1 to 4 (1 is the lowest and 4 is the highest).

I. **Basic Background Information**

   A. Computer Platform:
      IBM ___   Mac ✓

continued

B. System Requirements:
Stand Alone ___   Hard Drive Memory ✓
Networked ___   RAM Memory ✓
Both ___

C. Format (check one):
Disk-Based ✓
CD-ROM ___
Laserdisc ___

D. Audience:
PreK–1st ✓   9th–12th ___
2nd–5th ___   Adult ___
6th–8th ___   Other ___

E. Software Type:
CAI/Drill and Practice   ___
Simulations   ___
Problem-Solving Applications   ✓
Game Applications   ___
Tool Applications   ___
    Database   ___
    Word Processing   ___
    Spreadsheet   ___
Tutorials   ___
Grading/Student Information   ___
Electronic Portfolio Assessment   ___
Electronic Books   ___
    Skill level accommodations   ___
Multimedia authoring   ___
Telecommunicating   ___

F. Graphics: B/W ___ Color ✓ Animation ✓

G. Price: $375.00

H. Preview Policy: None ___ 30-day ✓ Other ___

II. Educational Objectives

A. State Purpose: To increase children's ability to hear phonemes within words

B. Subject Area Focus:
Math ___   Reading ✓   Art ___
Foreign Language ___   Social Studies ___ Science ___
Music ___   Literature ___   Other ___

III. Questions to Consider When Evaluating Software

A. Does the content of the program reflect a sound learning theory? If so, which one? Is the program's subject matter accurate and logically presented?
Yes. The program reflects Vygotsky's beliefs. The content is sequenced logically and is accurate.

B. Does the program promote exploration and critical thinking?
Yes. Children have to make decisions about phonemes while using specified criteria.

C. Does the software span a range of skill abilities?
No.

D. Do students have control of the program? (i.e., Is it self-paced? Can they navigate through the program easily?)
Yes.

E. Can the program be adapted to large groups, small groups, and individual instruction?
Yes.

F. Does the program accommodate different ability levels?
Yes.

G. Does the program provide supportive and positive feedback to students?
Yes.

H. Are teaching materials provided to accompany the program? If so, describe them.
Yes; puppets, games, rhymes, and stories to use in the classroom.

I. Is the program sensitive to multiculturalism? In what ways?
The program is neutral. It deals with sounds and letters.

J. Are the program directions clear enough to be used independently, or does the program require teacher support?
Requires teacher support initially and at identified sections prior to student self-pacing.

K. Does the school, classroom, or lab have the technical and educational support necessary to maximize the use of the program?
Yes.

L. Does the program have multimedia features? If so, do they enhance learning?
The program has multimedia features that increase the children's interest and motivation.

IV. **Rating (Rate items on a scale of 1 to 4; 4 is the highest.)**

A. Usability   4

B. Content   4

C. Design   4

D. Difficulty   4

Source: Designed by Jean Camp, Instructional Technology Coordinator, The University of North Carolina at Greensboro, Unpublished. Courtesy of Mary Olson, The University of North Carolina at Greensboro.

A Study of the School and School Services

An excellent way to get to know how a school functions and what services it provides to students is to conduct interviews of school personnel using an interview checklist. The procedures for good interviews discussed in Chapter Two of this guide, pages 35, 36, should be carefully followed.

SAMPLE FORM 23

Checklist for School Personnel Interviews

NAME OF INTERVIEWER: Ramona Machung

DATES OF INTERVIEWS: November 6, 20—December 20, 20—

SCHOOL: Mills River High School

OBJECTIVE OF OBSERVATION: To find out how a school functions and what services it provides

Instructions to the Interviewer: Schedule a conference with an appropriate person from each administrative division of the school. If a specific service is not identified, discuss with the principal or assistant principal how the school provides such a service or otherwise meets the needs of the students. Use checklists I–VI below to (1) formulate your questions and (2) ensure that you ask appropriate questions. You may add some of your own topics to the list. Check off each item for which you obtain an answer. Take notes in the space provided.

I.   Guidance, Testing, Evaluation, and Reporting

NAME OF PERSON INTERVIEWED: Mr. Armstrong

TITLE OF PERSON INTERVIEWED: Guidance Counselor

DATE, TIME, AND PLACE OF INTERVIEW: December 3, 20—, 11:30 a.m., Mr. Armstrong's office

APPROXIMATE LENGTH OF INTERVIEW: 15 minutes

- ✓ 1. Purpose of guidance program
- ✓ 2. Procedures for obtaining services
- ✓ 3. Services of guidance program (individual and group)
- ✓ 4. Referral services
- ✓ 5. Services for pregnant students and single parents
- ✓ 6. Teachers' role in guidance
- ✓ 7. Students' role in guidance
- ✓ 8. Parents' role in guidance
- ✓ 9. Standardized tests and purposes
- ✓ 10. School's grading/reporting policies
- ✓ 11. School's promotion/retention policies
- ✓ 12. Academic advising and placement of students

Notes:

Serves students, teachers, administrators, and parents. Works with administrators and teachers on academic, psychological, and social placement and testing of students.

Tests: Group and individual IQ tests, state competency tests, reading and Iowa Tests of Basic Skills. Individual students come for help with social/behavioral problems, help with scholarships, and college selection. Helped develop sexuality education classes and set up daycare for single parents. Worked with social workers regarding the health of pregnant girls.

II. Library or Media Center/Instructional Materials and Equipment

NAME OF PERSON INTERVIEWED: Mr. Andrade

TITLE OF PERSON INTERVIEWED: School Librarian/Media Specialist

DATE, TIME, AND PLACE OF INTERVIEW: December 6, 20—, 3:45 p.m., Library/Media Center

APPROXIMATE LENGTH OF INTERVIEW: 15 minutes

✓ 1. Available library materials related to subject and/or grade level
✓ 2. Library or media center hours for students and teachers
✓ 3. Procedures for using library or media center (class/students/teachers)
✓ 4. Vertical file and appropriate contents
✓ 5. Computer indexing of library materials
✓ 6. Equipment and media available for teachers' library/media center use
✓ 7. Checkout policies for students, teachers, and classes
✓ 8. Equipment and media available for classroom use
✓ 9. Procedures for instructing students in library/media center use
✓ 10. Assistance available for use of equipment and media
✓ 11. Availability and procedures for computer use by students and teachers
✓ 12. Procedures for selection and review of library materials and media

Notes:

Explained where fiction, nonfiction, and reference materials were for all curricular areas for sixth grade. Library open 8:10–3:30 daily for students, 7:30–4:30 for teachers. Both computer and vertical file indexing. Equipment: 3 movie projectors, 6 overhead projectors, 5 slide projectors, 1 opaque projector. Checked out first-come, first-served basis, but for 35 minutes at a time. Seven computers for student use in small room off media center. Chart of instructions about computer indexing and library and computer use.

III. Health Services

NAME OF PERSON INTERVIEWED: Mrs. Ginette Cortez

TITLE OF PERSON INTERVIEWED: Home-School Coordinator

DATE, TIME, AND PLACE OF INTERVIEW: December 13, 20—, 12:00 p.m., Health Clinic

APPROXIMATE LENGTH OF INTERVIEW: 20 minutes

✓ 1. Available health services at school
✓ 2. Services available through school referral
✓ 3. Sex education and condom distribution
✓ 4. Services for pregnant students
✓ 5. Procedures for teacher with ill/injured child
✓ 6. Procedures for dealing with HIV-positive student
✓ 7. School safety precautions, policies, and regulations
✓ 8. Other county/community services available to students
✓ 9. Health and related issues taught in classes

Notes:

First aid, cot for resting—eye and ear exams at community clinics. Flu shots at county clinic, work with guidance counselors, teachers on sexuality education—no condoms distributed as yet, but it has been discussed. School secretary calls parent/caregiver when child is ill at school. When HIV positive, refer for second opinion, student can come to classes. No smoking/drugs, guns, pushing, and running in halls allowed. Teach diet, nutrition, exercise, sexuality education.

continued

IV. Curriculum Resource Person or Assistant Principal for Curriculum

NAME OF PERSON INTERVIEWED: Mr. Roger Maldonado

TITLE OF PERSON INTERVIEWED: Assistant Principal

DATE, TIME, AND PLACE OF INTERVIEW: November 25, 20—, 9:15 a.m.,
Mr. Maldonado's office

APPROXIMATE LENGTH OF INTERVIEW: 30 minutes

✓ 1. School, district, county, or state curriculum guides
✓ 2. Multicultural aspects of the curriculum
✓ 3. School's organization for instruction:
  ✓ a. grouping
  ✓ b. departmentalization
  ✓ c. chain of command
  ✓ d. curricular offerings
  ✓ e. extracurricular offerings
  ✓ f. scheduling for teachers and students
✓ 4. Planning and reflection requirements for teachers
✓ 5. In-service and other opportunities for teachers
✓ 6. Observation and evaluation of teachers (Standards for Teaching, pp. 37–39)
✓ 7. Procedures for selection and review of textbooks and classroom materials
✓ 8. Teachers' role in curriculum development and implementation—May suggest ideas—not always implemented
✓ 9. Community's role in curriculum development and implementation—None
✓ 10. Procedures for dealing with controversial issues and/or materials—None
✓ 11. Special-education teachers
✓ 12. Reading teachers
✓ 13. Speech pathologists—None
✓ 14. Gifted-program teachers
✓ 15. Social-adjustment teachers, including drop-out prevention and in-school suspension—Started 1990–1991 year—seems to be helping
✓ 16. Dean of boys/girls—Yes
✓ 17. Music, art, and drama teachers—Yes—once a week
✓ 18. Other special teachers (bilingual, physical education)
✓ 19. Procedures for mainstreaming students

Notes:

Have county and state curriculum guides. Ability grouping for reading and mathematics, otherwise heterogeneous. Basic skills curriculum. Teachers plan week ahead, hand in plan books, planning time 30 min. daily. Principal observes new teachers 5 times a year; others 3 times—lets teachers know approximate days he will observe. Learning disability, reading, G.T. teachers. Students mainstreamed for music, art, social studies.

V. Person in Charge of Student Discipline

NAME OF PERSON INTERVIEWED: Mr. Roger Maldonado

TITLE OF PERSON INTERVIEWED: Vice Principal

DATE, TIME, AND PLACE OF INTERVIEW: December 16, 20—, 3:40 p.m.,
Mr. Maldonado's office

APPROXIMATE LENGTH OF INTERVIEW: 15 minutes

✓ 1. School policies/regulations regarding student behavior and appearance
✓ 2. Student handbook

✓ 3. Procedures for severe discipline referrals
✓ 4. Substance-abuse programs
✓ 5. Dropout prevention programs
✓ 6. School-administered discipline
✓ 7. Referrals to other agencies
✓ 8. Involvement of law enforcement in the school

Notes:

Policies on drugs, guns, crime, smoking, all substance abuse in student and parent handbooks. Discipline rules in all classrooms. Severe discipline problems referred to guidance counselor/principal/parent. Law officers can search lockers for suspected contents. When failing grades, placed in low student/teacher ratio—dropout prevention programs. School does not use corporal punishment as of this year. Have individual group therapy meetings with guidance counselor.

VI. Principal or Assistant Principal

NAME OF PERSON INTERVIEWED: Mrs. Elizabeth Andrews

TITLE OF PERSON INTERVIEWED: Principal

DATE, TIME, AND PLACE OF INTERVIEW: December 16, 20—, 4:30, Mrs. Andrew's office

APPROXIMATE LENGTH OF INTERVIEW: 40 minutes

✓ 1. School policies/regulations regarding teacher behavior and appearance
✓ 2. Faculty handbook Yes
✓ 3. Faculty meetings (time and how used) Weekly, 3:30, Discuss Parent's Day, Routines, Curriculum-Testing
✓ 4. Organizational pattern of local schools (i.e., board, central office, and/or school)
✓ 5. Specialized type of school, such as magnet
✓ 6. Specialized programs, such as before- and after-school programs and preschool or childcare programs
✓ 7. Information about the community served by the school
✓ 8. Community and parent involvement in the school
✓ 9. Business involvement in the school
✓ 10. Professional organizations (union and/or academic)
✓ 11. Teachers' extra responsibilities
✓ 12. Student employment opportunities and procedures to follow

Notes:

Appropriate, neat dress for males/females—may wear jeans, sweaters, sneakers. Teachers must sign in/out and be there from 7:30–4:15. There are 3 feeder elementary schools, 2 middle schools, and 1 high school served by one county-elected board of education. One elementary and one county middle school are magnet schools. There is a before- and after-school program. Breakfast is served to low-income families. Daycare provided for babies/young children of single teens. Teachers have bus, hall, and lunch duties. Children are bussed in across town for integration but still 65 percent white, 35 percent minority. Attendance at PTAs varies—if children involved most parents come. If it is a decision about playground expansion, raising money—about half come. Parents do respond to notes, some help with homework. Local business gave 20 computers and 10 typewriters. Most teachers belong to a professional organization as well as NEA or AFT and the state teacher's association. When ready to be certified, teachers need to complete application at county office, provide résumé, and make appointment with principal for an interview.

SAMPLE FORM 24

Reflective Observation of Classrooms, Schools, and Curriculum

NAME OF OBSERVER: Tiffany Johnson

DATE AND TIME OF OBSERVATION: May 24, 20—, 10:50 a.m.

TEACHER/SCHOOL: Mr. McCormack; Hargrove School

GRADE LEVEL AND/OR SUBJECT: Sixth Grade

OBJECTIVE OF OBSERVATION: To think carefully and reflect about your observation of classrooms, schools, and curriculum. Below are some guiding questions/statements related to each of the five steps in the reflection cycle (Chapter 1, pp. 9, 10, 11 of this guide). The questions/statements are directly related to the ten principles from the INTASC Standards (Chapter 2, pp. 37–39 of this guide).

Instructions to the Observer: Use Form 24A to respond to the following questions/statements when you have completed your observations.

1. **Select**
   a. What did you observe about the classroom that was different from and/or similar to your past experience?
   b. What did you observe about the school that was different from and/or similar to your past experience?
   c. What did you observe about the curriculum that was different from and/or similar to your past experience?
   d. What principles did you use from the INTASC Standards?

2. **Describe**
   a. Briefly describe your anecdotal observations of the school.
   b. Briefly describe your structured observation of strategies that challenge students' multiple intelligences.
   c. Did the school have the resources/materials that you expected it to have? Describe.

3. **Analyze**
   a. How has the curriculum changed since you were in elementary/high school?
   b. How did your observation of multicultural/antibias education compare/contrast to your own school experience?

4. **Appraise**
   a. What did you learn from these observations?
   b. How effective were you in completing the forms related to curriculum and technology?
   c. What sources of information about schools, classrooms, and curriculum were most helpful to you?

5. **Transform**
   a. What did you learn about technological resources that can help you in your teaching?
   b. What new knowledge and skills will you incorporate in your teaching?

Source: Adapted from North Carolina State Department of Public Instruction. *Performance Based Licensure.* Raleigh, NC, 1998–1999.

Chapter Four
Observing Students

Anecdotal Observations of Students

Anecdotal observations of students can reveal many things. One student can be observed over a long period of time in a variety of situations, or several different students can be observed on different occasions in the same classroom. Over a long period of time, changes can be seen in a student. It would be interesting to note, for example, differences in how Sammy, in the sample anecdotal record below, responds in his mathematics class of average-ability students as compared to his history class of above-average students. It would also be beneficial to note how his behavior in the history class changes from day to day and month to month. It might also be useful to observe several students of differing abilities in Sammy's history class. What is the ability level of Jennifer, the girl who helps Sammy? How does she respond in class? What are her interactions like with other students in the class? What about the boy who rolls his eyes at Sammy? What is his ability level, and how does he interact with other students?

SAMPLE FORM 25

Anecdotal Record for Observing Students

NAME OF OBSERVER: Sally Reider

DATE AND TIME OF OBSERVATION: October 18, 20—, 2:05–3:00 p.m.

LENGTH OF OBSERVATION: 55 minutes, one class period

PERSON AND/OR EVENT OBSERVED: Sammy Hayes, student

GRADE LEVEL AND/OR SUBJECT: Tenth grade; American History

OBJECTIVE OF OBSERVATION: To see how an average-ability tenth grader responds in a history classroom

Instructions to the Observer: Write a detailed account of your subject, noting his or her appearance, background, abilities, interaction with others, habits, class responsiveness, behavior, and so on. Try to be as objective as possible.

According to his teacher, Sammy Hayes is an average-ability tenth grader. Although he is average in ability based on standardized test scores, Sammy is one of those students who works diligently. I am observing Sammy's tenth-grade history classroom. His teacher suggested that today would be a good day to observe Sammy because the students are working in small groups, and Sammy usually contributes well to the group. So that Sammy does not know I am particularly observing him, I will sit outside the group, but in a place where I can hear the students's interactions.

The bell rings. Sammy comes into the room quietly. The teacher pointed Sammy out to me yesterday so that I could quickly spot him. He's an average-looking kid: average height, slight build, teenage complexion (but no acne), medium-length brown hair—looks a bit greasy today. His clothes are typical, too: bleached blue jeans and a white T-shirt, running shoes without socks. Sammy does not stand out. He is neither attractive nor unattractive. Although he does not appear to be particularly outgoing, he is also not shy. He looks like the kind of kid who could easily get lost.

He sits down at his desk while many of the students mill around the room, but he is not a loner. He is talking to the boy sitting next to him, and the girl in front has turned around to ask him something. It appears she's asking him something about the assignment, since she's finding a page in his textbook.

The bell rings. Most of the students go to their seats. The teacher must remind a few of them that it's time to sit down. Sammy continues to talk quietly to the girl in front of him, but looks up and becomes quiet when the teacher looks at the class and says, "All right, class, today we're going to work in our groups to prepare for our oral presentations. But, before we do so, hand your homework up to the person in the seat in front of you. "Yes, Sammy?" Sammy says, "Katie and I were just talking about our homework, and we don't know what numbers we were supposed to do. I thought it was 1, 3, and 7 and Katie thought it was 1, 3, and 9." A boy in the front says, "That's because we had a choice for the last question!" "That's right," the teacher says to Sammy, "You and Katie are both right. Now will you hand in your homework?" Sammy hands his to Katie.

I should probably say here that Sammy's teacher told me that this is a college prep class, and Sammy is one of the less able students in the class, but he tries so hard that the guidance office decided to place him in it. However, the teacher says he thinks Sammy is beginning to get frustrated. For all his trying, he's only getting C's. In his other, less competitive classes, he gets A's.

The teacher tells the students to get in their groups as they did on Monday and to have one group member go to the bookshelves and pick up the material they were working on. He reminds them that they should take all their material with them and move only the desks nearest where their group is supposed to meet. He also reminds them that this group project counts for a third of their grade for this unit. These are good kids and they follow his instructions, although there seems to be some confusion at the bookshelves. The teacher goes over to straighten it out.

Sammy has moved to his group and is asking another student what they are supposed to be doing today. The student rolls his eyes and says, "We're supposed to finish what we started on Monday." Sammy still looks puzzled, but doesn't pursue it.

The room is noisy, and the teacher says, "O.K., folks, you should have your materials. Now, get back to your group and get started. If you have questions, have one group member raise a hand and I'll get to you as soon as I can." Three groups already have hands up. No one in Sammy's group has raised a hand.

The girl who was getting the group's materials returns to Sammy's group and begins to hand things out from the box she has picked up. She gives Sammy a book. Sammy frowns. "What am I supposed to do with this?" he says. "Wait, Sammy," the girl says, "We haven't started yet." Most of the group members begin looking things up. One boy is drawing a map of what appears to be a battlefield. Several others are talking and laughing. Sammy is just sitting, staring at the book. Leadership seems to be lacking in this group. Finally, one of the boys says to Sammy, "Hey, Sammy, you're supposed to be looking up information about the Battle of Gettysburg." Sammy's eyes light up in recognition, and he immediately gets busy. I can't help but notice that he does not appear to know how to look things up in an index; he's

continued

looking in the table of contents. After some time, he finds an appropriate chapter and turns to it. He begins thumbing through the chapter. When he finally finds something, he calls out, "Wow, did you know how many Union soldiers were killed at Gettysburg?" One student looks over Sammy's shoulder at the passage and says, "Wow!" Another student says, "Sammy, you're supposed to be writing those things down. Remember the hand-out from Monday? You need to fill it out so we can compile all the information for our chart. Remember?" "Oh, yeah," says Sammy. He begins looking for the sheet. The girl who'd looked over his shoulder says, "I think it's in the box, Sammy; mine was." Sammy goes to the box to look and finds his sheet way on the bottom. His name is on it, but little else. Several of the students who are doing other battles are nearly through. Sammy begins diligently searching. Some of the other students begin to report their data to put on the chart. One boy says to Sammy, "Who was the commanding officer for the South at Gettysburg?" Sammy says, "I haven't found that yet." The boy rolls his eyes, but the girl next to Sammy says, "I've finished most of mine; your battle is harder. Let me help you look for it." Sammy smiles, and they begin to work together. The teacher walks by, sees the group is working, and starts to move on. He looks at Sammy's paper and sees that he's barely begun. "What's the problem, Sammy?" he asks. Sammy shrugs. "Can I help?" the teacher asks. "No, I can do it," Sammy says, looking down. The girl says to the teacher, "Sammy's got the hardest battle; I'll help him because I finished." "Thank you, Jennifer," the teacher says. (I like this Jennifer girl; I'll need to ask the teacher about her.) Sammy and Jennifer continue to work together. Sammy is now smiling. The rest of the group is ignoring them as they continue to list on the chart facts from the other battles.

(The observation continues in this fashion.)

Shadowing a Student

A simple, but time-consuming, anecdotal technique for determining what it is like to be a particular student in a particular school is shadowing that student throughout an entire school day. From this process, the observer can learn how the student interacts with teachers and other students. In addition, the preservice teacher can discover how the student handles social and academic situations and what the student does with his or her non-class time. Most important, the observer can learn what a day in the life of a student in a particular school is like.

Before shadowing a student, it is essential to obtain permission from the student, since shadowing is an intrusion into his or her life. The teacher(s) of the student, the principal, and, in some cases, the student's parents or guardians should also grant permission. The observer should carefully explain that the goal of shadowing is not to analyze the individual, but rather to determine what it is like to be a student at his or her school. The observer should encourage the student to behave as naturally as possible, explaining that shadowing will not be as helpful to the observer if he or she acts differently than usual or tells his or her friends about the observation. The observer should ask the student to try to ignore him as much as possible and simply follow his or her schedule, remaining as unobtrusive as possible.

In classrooms, the observer should sit out of the line of sight of the majority of the students. In the lunchroom, the observer should sit where the student can be observed, but where the observer cannot be seen by the student. If possible, the observer should talk with the student at the end of the day, sharing observations, not judgments, and asking about the student's perception of school, peers, subjects, likes, and dislikes. A separate shadowing form should be completed for each lesson and/or separate time period (i.e., classes, lunch, and recess) during the day.

According to a study on the values of shadowing students, researchers Melody Jones and Martin Tadlock concluded, "As you follow students around you begin to feel you are one of them. You see yourself through their eyes. It is an unsettling type of introspection. You have to shrink, you have to think like a student. If you're really interested in understanding students, a shadow study is a good way to do it" (1999, 61).

SAMPLE FORM 26

Shadowing Form

NAME OF SHADOWED STUDENT: Natasha Reynolds*

NAME OF OBSERVER: Sally Burke

DATE AND TIME OF SHADOW: September 4, 20—, 8:30–10:20

GRADE LEVEL AND/OR SUBJECT: Twelfth grade; German/English

OBJECTIVE OF SHADOW: To understand what it is like to be a student at East Rodgers High School

GENERAL DESCRIPTION OF LOCATION: Classrooms: German II/German III—28 students (8 girls, 20 boys); English—30 students (16 girls, 14 boys)

*The name of the shadowed student and the school have been changed.

Instructions to the Observer: Select a student to shadow for an entire school day. Use a separate page for each class period or segment of the school day you observe. Every five to fifteen minutes, record what the subject of the observation is doing; also indicate what other students and teachers are doing. At the end of the day, summarize the shadowing experience. If possible, interview the student and report the results.

SUBJECT/CLASS: German

Time (recorded every five to fifteen minutes)	What Subject Was Doing	What Classmates and Teacher Were Doing
8:30–8:35	Talking to neighbor	T. told class to be quiet for morning announcements. Most students talked.
8:35–8:45	Translated sentence into literal English—sounded bizarre	T. tried to help students correct quiz from day before. T. told personal anecdotes. Most of class amused.
8:45–8:50	Put head on desk	"
8:50–9:00	Answered question	"
9:00–9:10	Talked to neighbor; put head down	"

continued

SUBJECT/CLASS: English

Time	What Subject Was Doing	What Classmates and Teacher Were Doing
9:20–9:35	Worked on quiz	T. gave quiz on assignment. All but one student worked diligently. He didn't write any answers.
9:35–9:40	Answered question # 4	T. let students correct own papers.
9:40–9:45	Head down on desk	
9:45–9:50	Appeared to listen to others reading orally	Students took turns reading orally.
9:50–10:00	Read silently, put head down, then up, then read again	T. gave directions to read William Bradford's "Of Plymouth Plantation." Most students read quietly; some talked.
10:00–10:10	Answered two questions about what she had read	T. asked questions about content of silent reading. Most students knew the answers. T. paraphrased what students had read.
10:10	Closed book: got out of seat	T. assigned questions in text for homework.

The following should be completed at the end of the shadowing experience:

1. **Overview:** Summarize how the student seemed to be involved, how the student interacted with teachers and peers, what the student seemed to learn, and how the student
seems to feel about the class.
Overview—Natasha didn't appear to be that interested in the German class. I got the
impression from Natasha that she took the class because she thought it would be easy
for her since her mother is German. She was more attentive in the English class, especially
when she could answer questions. She did seem to lose some interest when reading silently.

2. **Report of interview with student:**
(Lunch time outside on picnic table)—Natasha asked me several questions about college. She said she'd like to go there someday. She said history and English were her
favorite subjects, but not her favorite classes. Her major complaint about school was
not enough time for lunch or in between classes to socialize. Natasha said she liked
horses and someday hopes to own and manage a rehabilitation horse barn.

Anecdotal Profile of a Student

The anecdotal profile technique is similar to, but less time-consuming than, shadowing. It
allows the observer to study two or more students during a single lesson.

The goal of the anecdotal profile is to examine the attitudes and activities of several students during a specified period of time. The observer should select two or three students to
observe for fifteen to twenty minutes each. It is helpful if these students are quite different in
terms of certain key characteristics (e.g., appearance, sociability, or academic achievement).
Because the observation of the students is for a limited time period, the observer should record
the students' activities and attitudes every one to two minutes, rather than every five minutes
as in the shadowing study. These observations can be kept on three-by-five-inch index cards.

SAMPLE FORM 27.1

Profile Card of Student 1

NAME OF OBSERVER: Monica Williams

STUDENT: Jason Maxwell

DATE AND TIME OF OBSERVATION: December 5, 20—, 9:30–9:40 a.m.

GRADE LEVEL AND/OR SUBJECT: Third grade; reading group of 5

LOCATION: Classroom

OBJECTIVE OF OBSERVATION: To examine the attitude and activities of a particular student

Instructions to the Observer: Record your observations in five minute intervals.

Time (recorded every five minutes)	Student's Activities/Attitudes
9:30–9:35	Adjusts chair; moves body left to right; whispers to friend next to him on his left.
9:35–9:40	Looks at reading chart; raises hand. Stands up, responds, "Divide between the two consonants."
9:40–9:45	Raises hand again when not called on, says, "I knew that, too." Plays with book on lap.
9:45–9:50	Opens book; appears to be reading silently; sometimes moves lips.
9:50–9:55	Raises hand again and says, "I know, I know." When not called on, appears to sulk.

SAMPLE FORM 27.2

Profile Card of Student 2

NAME OF OBSERVER: Monica Williams

STUDENT: Maggie Reid

DATE AND TIME OF OBSERVATION: December 5, 20—, 9:45–10:00 a.m.

GRADE LEVEL AND/OR SUBJECT: Third grade; reading group of 5

LOCATION: Classroom

OBJECTIVE OF OBSERVATION: To examine the attitude and activities of a particular student

continued

Instructions to the Observer: Record your observations in five minute intervals.

Time (recorded every five minutes)	Student's Activities/Attitudes
9:45–9:50	Raises hand; says: "The boy wanted to help the old man." Smiles at person on her right. Plays with hair, makes noise with her shoes.
9:50–9:55	Appears to listen to others's responses. Plays with her hair. Asks, "Can I read that part out loud?"
9:55–10:00	Closes book; puts it under chair. Picks up workbook and pencil. Turns pages looking for right page. Scowls and says, "We did this before."
10:00–10:05	Takes pencil; puts an X after phrases in book. Works fast and says, "It's the same, but different."

Structured Observation of Students

There are many types of structured observations that can reveal specific information about students. Descriptive profile charts are more specific and focused than the anecdotal profiles discussed previously. Checklists are very specific, allowing the observer to focus on a specified list of items. A checklist does not evaluate, it documents. Coding systems allow observers to tally elements of student behavior. Informal inventories of students allow observers to gain data about students from the students' perspectives. Sociograms assist observers in plotting the interaction of students in a social environment such as a classroom.

Descriptive Profiles of a Student

Descriptive profiles are very similar to anecdotal profiles; however, they are more complete in that they attempt to record a continuing collection of facts in order to describe a particular phenomenon. The recordings are made without regard to their meaning, value, or use. A descriptive profile always begins with the date, time, and place, and includes statements and explanations about the background of the situation or setting. Descriptions tell what happened, who did or said what, and how it was done. They are noted as objectively and completely as possible. Direct quotes are recorded, posture and facial expressions are described, and gestures and voice quality are noted. However, interpretations are avoided. Thus a detailed, descriptive sentence such as "His eyes flashed, he frowned, his body became rigid, and his fist was clenched," seeks to state the facts, while a biased statement such as "He was angry" (Perkins, 1969, 28), seeks to interpret the facts and should be avoided. The descriptive profile is a lot like what a writer attempts to do when setting a scene in a literary work. The author attempts to show the readers the scene to make the readers feel as if they are there. The author attempts to keep out of the scene, and, therefore, shows rather than tells. The descriptive profile should do the same thing.

In descriptive profiles, observations should be limited to only a few phenomena at a time. Descriptive observers can make their jobs easier by looking for specific elements of a personality or environment. For example, the descriptive profile chart that follows outlines one student's actions during a lesson. The observer is looking for how and when the student is actively involved in the lesson and how and when she is not.

SAMPLE FORM 28

Descriptive Profile Chart

PLOTTED BY: Sarah Cardinalli

DATE AND TIME OF OBSERVATION: October 28, 20—, 8:45 a.m.

STUDENT: Melissa Hernandez

SCHOOL: Smith Elementary

GRADE LEVEL: Second grade

INTERVAL: Twenty seconds

OBJECTIVE OF OBSERVATION: To record a student's involvement or lack of involvement in two different activities of a lesson

Instructions to the Observer: Record brief phrases to indicate the activities of the student during discussion and work periods. Place student activities under "application" if they show involvement in the lesson; if not, place them under "distraction".

DISCUSSION PERIOD		WORK PERIOD	
Application	**Distraction**	**Application**	**Distraction**
Listened to teacher.		Opened workbook. Looked at work.	
Raised hand.	Fiddled with pencil.	Frowned.	
Listened, shook head.			Doodled. Talked to neighbor.
	Played with fingernails.		
Looked at book.		Looked at workbook. Raised hand.	Frowned.
Answered question.			Doodled.
		Listened to teacher.	
Asked question.		Looked at book.	
Read assignment on board.			Played with fingernails.
	Looked at fingernails.	Picked up pencil.	
	Talked to student next to her.	Wrote in book.	Frowned.
Looked at teacher; raised hand.			Put head on desk.
	Looked at student.		
Asked question.			
Listened to answer.			

Source: Adapted from John Devor. *The Experience of Student Teaching,* 1964.

Coding Systems of Student Participation

Another simple tool to help observers limit what they are looking for in a classroom is the coding system. A coding system looks for specific elements within the classroom. Usually the observer codes the extent of the presence of these elements on three-by-five-inch index cards. The technique is most frequently used when observing students and teachers. Just as with other observational tools, the observers must know what they are looking for before designing the coding system.

In the example of a coding system below, the observer is looking for the extent of participation of various students in the lesson. Cards could be made to record the participation of several students during a single lesson. Over a period of time, all students' participation could be coded.

SAMPLE FORM 29

Coding System to Observe Student Participation in Lessons

NAME OF OBSERVER: Sally Reider

DATE AND TIME OF OBSERVATION: October 18, 20—, 10:45

STUDENT: Sammy Hayes

GRADE LEVEL: Tenth grade

TOPIC: Civil War

OBJECTIVE OF OBSERVATION: To observe the extent of a student's participation in a particular lesson

Instructions to the Observer: Place a slash [/] in the appropriate column to indicate student activities during a single lesson.

Important Contributions	Minor Contributions	Distracting Remarks
//	⧵⧵⧵⧵ /	///

Informal Inventories of Students

Another simple technique for gathering data about students is developing inventories that list the interests of students, their favorite teachers, how students view themselves, how they view the school, and the subjects they take. Almost anything the observer wants to learn about the students can be asked on an informal inventory. Many inventories are available through educational publications. However, the inventories that are the most valuable to observers are those designed to meet the objectives of the specific class. What follows is a simple interest inventory, designed by a student observer, to determine the student's interest in reading. Inventories can also be administered to a large group of students and tallied to learn the most common responses. You are encouraged to design an inventory appropriate to the objectives of a specific student or class.

SAMPLE FORM 30

Incomplete Sentence Inventory

OBSERVER'S NAME: Irene Johnson

DATE AND TIME OF OBSERVATION: September 13, 20—, 2:00 p.m.

STUDENT: Billy Malone

GRADE LEVEL AND/OR SUBJECT: Fourth grade; reading

OBJECTIVE OF OBSERVATION: To determine Billy's reading interests

Instructions to the Observer: Determine the purpose of completing an informal inventory. Then design some incomplete sentences related to your objective. A sample answer for the first question should be provided in the instructions to the student. Observer can read incomplete sentences to children who are unable to read.

Instructions to the Student: Complete each sentence as honestly and completely as possible. For example, you might complete the first questions as follows: When I get home from school I usually play outside.

1. When I get home from school I usually get a snack.
2. On rainy Saturdays I particularly like to do puzzles.
3. When I am at home in the summer, I like to play ball.
4. When I go to the beach or pool, I always take with me my ball, my friend, Jim.
5. When I was a small child I remember my mother read to me.
6. When I was a small child I remember my father _____. (Billy did not complete this sentence.)
7. The best book I remember reading is about snakes.
8. I like to read the magazine National Geographic.
9. The last book I read was The Fascinating World of Bees.

Peer Group Interaction: Sociograms

For most students, their interaction with peers is exceedingly important. In fact, by middle or junior-high school, interaction with peers takes precedence over all other interactions. Therefore, it is helpful to discover ways to observe and analyze how students relate to one other. Perhaps the easiest technique for accomplishing this is the sociogram.

A sociogram graphically examines how the students in a class feel about one another. It indicates which students are most liked by other students and which are isolated from other students. Completing the sociogram requires the cooperation of the classroom teacher.

To complete a simple sociogram, the observer or the classroom teacher should have students list three classmates with whom they would like to be socially associated. For example, students can be told, "On our field trip next week, we will be in groups of four. Please list three other students, in order of preference, that you'd most like to be grouped with for the trip." It should be made clear to students that the teacher cannot guarantee that all their suggestions will be followed, but their preferences will be used as a guide in helping to form the groups. The students' choices can be tallied on a chart such as Sample Form 31. The names of students in the class are listed both vertically and horizontally. Those students who are in the vertical list are considered choosers. The order in which they have selected companions is given in the horizontal box next to the person's name. At the bottom of the form is a place to tally the total number of choices per student.

SAMPLE FORM 31

Tally Chart of Student-Group Selections

NAME OF OBSERVER: Danny McKinney

DATE AND TIME OF OBSERVATION: October 26, 20—, 1:00 p.m.

SCHOOL: Eastfield Middle School

OBJECTIVE OF OBSERVATION: To determine which students are most liked and which students are most isolated

Instructions to the Observer: List students on left side. Then tally the first, second, and third choices made by each student in the chart below.

Chosen / Choosers	Pam	John*	David	Steve	George	Brian G.	Paul	Scott F.	Scott K.	Jeff	Ruth	Marc	Libby	Sherman	Sharon	Tony	Judy	Alan	Brian S.	Jane	Wayne	Bill	Keith	Sandy	Lane
Pam													1		2		3								
John*																									
David				3	2											1									
Steve					1														3					2	
George											1					2					3				
Brian G.		1														2						3			
Paul											1	2									3				
Scott F.						2				1											3				
Scott K.							2									3							1		
Jeff				3															2			1			
Ruth												1									3				2
Marc						1											2	3							
Libby	3						2																	1	
Sherman							2									1					3				
Sharon	3									1						2									
Tony			1	2																	3				
Judy	3																	1							2
Alan							1												2		3				
Brian S.							2									1					3				
Jane				3							1	2													
Wayne							2					1						3							
Bill							2	3															1		
Keith		2		3																					
Sandy							2					1									3				
Lane												1						2						3	
Chosen 1		1	1			1	2		1	3	4	2		1	2	1						3	1	1	1
Chosen 2		1				2	7				1	1			1	2	2	1	2				1		2
Chosen 3	3			3	1				1							1	1	1	2		4	1		1	
Totals	3	2	1	3	2	3	9	0	1	1	3	5	3	0	2	5	3	3	4	0	9	4	2	2	2

* John absent

Source: Frederick J. McDonald. *Educational Psychology*, 2nd ed., Wadsworth Publishing, 1965, 634.

In order to graphically illustrate which students are more socially popular than others, a sociogram can be constructed based on the information obtained in the tally chart. In Sample Form 32, for example, boys are drawn in circles, girls in squares. Arrows are drawn to each student selected, with the number of his or her selection marked as first, second, or third. Dotted lines indicate those students who selected one another. The larger circles and squares represent those who were selected more often than others.

SAMPLE FORM 32

Sociogram Based on Charted Student Preferences

NAME OF OBSERVER: *Rebecca Talmadge*

DATE AND TIME OF OBSERVATION: *October 30, 20—, 2:00 p.m.*

SCHOOL: *Faircrest Elementary School*

GRADE LEVEL AND/OR SUBJECT: *Fourth grade*

OBJECTIVE OF OBSERVATION: *To illustrate children's choices in pictorial, graphic format, showing students most liked and those most isolated*

Instructions to the Observer: Use the tally chart of student-group selections to put the names of the most-selected students in a prominent place on the page. Identify males by placing their names in circles, females by placing their names in boxes. Then, put the names of students selected by those few most-selected students next to them. If they selected each other, connect them with a dotted line. If not, draw an arrow to the student selected. Proceed in this fashion until all names are represented on the form.

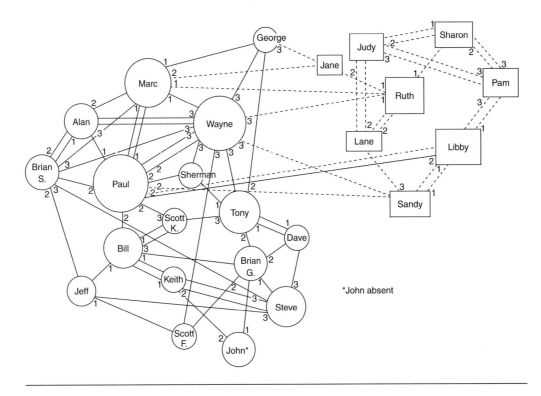

Source: Frederick J. McDonald. *Educational Psychology,* 2nd ed., Wadsworth Publishing, 1965, 635.

If special students, including the disabled and gifted, are included in regular classrooms, the school is responsible for creating both an environment and an Individual Educational Plan (IEP) that will allow each special student to succeed. To ensure student success, it is necessary to determine the needs of each student and to create within the classroom the least restrictive environment possible so that the special student can participate academically and socially and can achieve.

SAMPLE FORM 33

Reasonable Public School Expectations for Students

NAME OF OBSERVER: Sophia Hoosain

DATE AND TIME OF OBSERVATION: October 18, 20—, 9:00 a.m.

SCHOOL/TEACHER: Highland Elementary, Mr. Byrd

STUDENT: Tikamiya Owen

GRADE LEVEL AND/OR SUBJECT: Fifth grade; self-contained

AREA OF IDENTIFICATION (DISABILITY, IF KNOWN):   Blind

OBJECTIVE OF OBSERVATION: To determine the extent to which a disabled student is successful in three developmental areas

Instructions to the Observer: What follows is a checklist of reasonable performance and behavior that teachers can expect from nondisabled students. In order to develop an Individual Educational Plan (IEP) for a disabled student, it is necessary to determine which of these expectations he or she is able to meet with no curriculum or classroom modifications. In the right-hand column, indicate the extent to which the student is successful in each of these categories. Note that some of this information may be available only from the student's academic file or teacher; it is important that you make no assumptions and obtain appropriate documentation.

Developmental Areas	Very	Moderate	Limited	None
A. Academic Development				
1. Reading	✔			
2. Writing		✔		
3. Mathematics	✔			
B. Social Development				
1. Interaction with other students		✔		
2. Interaction with teacher or other staff	✔			
C. Physical Development				
1. Uses regular transportation to school; walks or rides school bus				✔
2. Reports to homeroom or other central location by her/himself			✔	
3. Obeys school rules with other students	✔			
4. Goes to class with regular curriculum				
a. regular volume of curriculum	✔			
b. regular rate of presentation of material	✔			
c. at a reading level that is grade-level appropriate	✔			
5. Has homework assignments in every class		✔		
6. Changes classes when the bell rings			✔	
7. Mingles in hallway before next class			✔	

continued

Developmental Areas		Very	Moderate	Limited	None
8.	Has lunch with other youngsters		✔		
9.	Goes to gym/PE with other youngsters		✔		
10.	Dresses for gym/PE			✔	
11.	Goes to the restroom as classes change	✔			
12.	Has recess/free time with others		✔		
13.	Attends regular school assemblies	✔			
14.	Takes regular tests without modifications			✔	
15.	Participates in extracurricular activities		✔		
16.	Goes on school field trips or outings	✔			
17.	Does homework each night		✔		
18.	Takes homework back to teacher each day		✔		
19.	Attends school each day with very few excused absences	✔			
20.	Makes up work if absent		✔		

Source: Adapted from a form used by the Asheville, North Carolina, public schools.

SAMPLE FORM 34

Information-Processing Categories of Instructional Modifications

NAME OF OBSERVER: Sophia Hoosain

DATE AND TIME OF OBSERVATION: October 20, 20—, 12:30 p.m.

SCHOOL/TEACHER: Highland Elementary, Mr. Byrd

STUDENT: Tikamiya Owen

GRADE LEVEL AND/OR SUBJECT: Fifth grade; self-contained

AREA OF IDENTIFICATION (DISABILITY, IF KNOWN):   Blind

OBJECTIVE OF OBSERVATION: To observe instructional modifications made in a regular classroom for a disabled student

Instructions to the Observer: What follows is a checklist of modifications targeted to the disabled student. Any variety of these modifications may be needed in order for a disabled student to be successful in the school or classroom environment and/or to achieve curricular goals. Observe a disabled student who is in the regular classroom and check [✔] those modifications that are currently being employed. If a modification is needed but is not currently employed, place an asterisk [*] to the left of the item.

Note: It may be necessary to interview the classroom teacher to determine whether some of these items are currently employed.

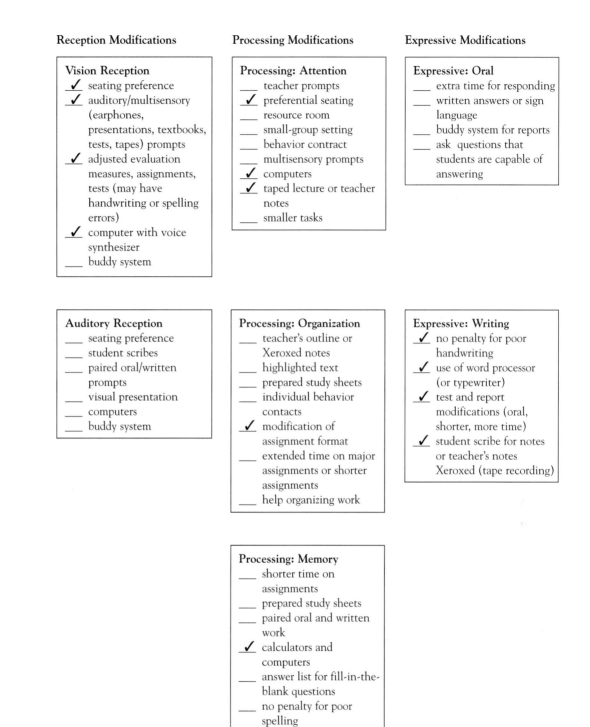

Reception Modifications

Vision Reception
- ✔ seating preference
- ✔ auditory/multisensory (earphones, presentations, textbooks, tests, tapes) prompts
- ✔ adjusted evaluation measures, assignments, tests (may have handwriting or spelling errors)
- ✔ computer with voice synthesizer
- ___ buddy system

Auditory Reception
- ___ seating preference
- ___ student scribes
- ___ paired oral/written prompts
- ___ visual presentation
- ___ computers
- ___ buddy system

Processing Modifications

Processing: Attention
- ___ teacher prompts
- ✔ preferential seating
- ___ resource room
- ___ small-group setting
- ___ behavior contract
- ___ multisensory prompts
- ✔ computers
- ✔ taped lecture or teacher notes
- ___ smaller tasks

Processing: Organization
- ___ teacher's outline or Xeroxed notes
- ___ highlighted text
- ___ prepared study sheets
- ___ individual behavior contacts
- ✔ modification of assignment format
- ___ extended time on major assignments or shorter assignments
- ___ help organizing work

Processing: Memory
- ___ shorter time on assignments
- ___ prepared study sheets
- ___ paired oral and written work
- ✔ calculators and computers
- ___ answer list for fill-in-the-blank questions
- ___ no penalty for poor spelling

Expressive Modifications

Expressive: Oral
- ___ extra time for responding
- ___ written answers or sign language
- ___ buddy system for reports
- ___ ask questions that students are capable of answering

Expressive: Writing
- ✔ no penalty for poor handwriting
- ✔ use of word processor (or typewriter)
- ✔ test and report modifications (oral, shorter, more time)
- ✔ student scribe for notes or teacher's notes Xeroxed (tape recording)

Source: Adapted from a form used by the Asheville, North Carolina, public schools: *Reception Modifications.*

SAMPLE FORM 35

Reflective Observation of Students

NAME OF OBSERVER: Angela Sexton

DATE AND TIME OF REFLECTIVE RECORD: April 26, 20—, 1:15 p.m.

TEACHER/SCHOOL: Mr. Santuro, South Central Academy

GRADE LEVEL AND/OR SUBJECT: Twelfth grade; physics

OBJECTIVE OF OBSERVATION: To think carefully and reflect about your observation of students. Below are some guiding questions/statements related to each of the five steps in the reflection cycle (Chapter One, pp. 9, 10, 11). The statements are directly related to the ten principles from the INTASC Standards (Chapter Two, pp. 37, 38, 39).

Instructions to the Observer: Use Form 35A to respond to the following questions after you have completed your observations.

1. **Select**
   a. What anecdotal observations of students did you complete?
   b. What structured observation of students did you complete?
   c. What principles from INTASC Standards did you address?

2. **Describe**
   a. What are the unique characteristics that distinguish these students from others you have observed (e.g., needs, background, learning styles, prior experiences)?
   b. What steps did you take to assess the needs of these students?
   c. From whom and in what ways did you solicit information about the students' experiences, learning behaviors, and needs?

3. **Analyze**
   a. How will your assessment of the characteristics and needs of these students affect your planning, tutoring, and teaching?
   b. How did the cultural, ethnic, and racial characteristics of these students influence you and your interactions with them?

4. **Appraise**
   a. What sources of information were most helpful to you as you consider planning and teaching these students?
   b. What observation(s) improved your understanding of the diverse needs of students at this age/grade?

5. **Transform**
   a. What did you learn about the diverse nature and needs of students?
   b. What new knowledge and skills will you incorporate in your teaching?

Source: Adapted from North Carolina State Department of Public Instruction. *Performance Based Licensure.* Raleigh, NC, 1998–1999.

PART III

Developing Successful Teaching Skills

Chapter Five

Participation: Preteaching and Planning

Preteaching Activities

Working in classrooms should proceed in a series of gradual steps from observation to teaching. After teacher-education students have had the opportunity to observe and reflect on their observations, they can ease into their roles as teachers by assisting the classroom teacher in a variety of noninstructional or teacher-aide duties. When the preservice teacher has mastered some of these duties, he or she can begin working with the teacher in the ongoing instructional activity of the classroom. Still later, the teacher-education student can begin to assume some limited teaching assignments that are carefully planned with the classroom teacher, such as individual tutoring and small-group instructional work. Not until the preservice teacher feels comfortable with these activities and has had time to reflect upon them and receive feedback about them should he or she move on to assume primary responsibility for a fully planned lesson. Before teaching the lesson, careful planning with the classroom teacher is essential. This step-by-step process will be discussed in the remaining chapters.

After observing and before teaching, there are numerous activities that can help student participants better understand the children, the classroom organization, and the teaching process. Lani, in the anecdotal observation in Chapter 1, discussed some of these: taking roll, bringing his pet mice to class, discussing teaching techniques with the classroom teacher, etc. Janet Joyce, in the anecdotal record of preteaching activities in this chapter, discusses others: helping the children with art projects, going to staff-development meetings, taking field trips, putting up a bulletin board, working with the teacher-aide to develop a classroom management system, discussing students with the teacher and teaching specialists, and filling out a worksheet related to a field trip students had taken. The first section of this chapter will provide you with additional ideas for preteaching activities. Tools for planning will be discussed in the second section of the chapter.

SAMPLE FORM 36

Anecdotal Record of Preteaching Activities

STUDENT: Janet Joyce

TEACHER: Ms. Bennes

GRADE LEVEL: Second grade

continued

DATE: February 11, 20— to March 15, 20—

OBJECTIVE: To record activities I participated in prior to teaching

Instructions to Student Participant: Keep an account of the activities you participated in prior to actual teaching. Indicate how you felt about each day's events.

FEBRUARY 11, 20—

The thing I liked most about today was helping the kids with their valentine folders. I had never woven paper before. It was fun watching them do it. It was a great first day!

FEBRUARY 12, 20—

School was dismissed early for staff development. The kids were pretty excited about it. Ms. Bennes and I spent the afternoon talking with Ms. Loritch, the speech teacher, about several of our students.

FEBRUARY 13, 20—

Today was a full day! We went on a field trip to the Health Adventure. The kids learned a lesson on dental hygiene. It was great and the kids liked it too. This afternoon we had a surprise birthday party for Ms. Canty, the teacher-aide. The kids never gave the secret away (which was a miracle). Ms. Canty was surprised and the party went well.

FEBRUARY 14, 20—

The whole day was great! I helped the kids make their valentines and showed them the proper way to address them. They counted valentine candy. This afternoon they had their valentine party. It was fun, but I'll be glad when things get back to normal.

FEBRUARY 19, 20—

I found a worksheet called "Dental Insurance." I think it would be a neat activity to do as a follow-up to the Health Adventure field trip. There is math included on the worksheet. The students have to figure out the math problem in order to know what color to color a part of the picture. They will then write a letter to Dr. Trueluck, thanking him for paying their way to the Health Adventure. The letter is on the back of the picture.

FEBRUARY 20, 20—

We went on another field trip this morning. We went to see the Elephant Walk downtown. (The circus came to town.) We walked to get there. I never knew how tiring it could be to walk five blocks with 16 kids. By the end of the day, I was so tired that I didn't think I would make it home. But I did, and I was sure glad to be there.

FEBRUARY 21, 20—

I taught my first spelling lesson today. It went O.K. I think it could have been better. I never taught a spelling lesson before, and I basically did it the way Ms. Bennes does. It just wasn't me. Maybe tomorrow will be a little better.

FEBRUARY 22, 20—

Today's lesson went a little better. I can still see where there can be a lot of improvement. I'm going to have to sit down and really think of a different twist to teaching spelling.

FEBRUARY 25, 20—

Today was pretty bad. The kids didn't want to listen, and they didn't. This afternoon I read a story to them, and they were all over the place. Ms. Bennes even said she had not seen them act this way before. Ms. Bennes and I talked to the ones who were misbehaving. I just can't imagine another day like this one.

FEBRUARY 26, 20—

Today was so much better! They listened, they were polite, they were almost little sweethearts. We did something different in spelling that they seemed to enjoy, and I think that helped a lot. This was a great turnaround from yesterday.

MARCH 6, 20—

Today we had a statewide tornado drill. It was supposed to be at 9:30, but it wasn't until about 10:15. It made the morning very disorganized, and we really didn't get a whole lot accomplished. This afternoon, I will help some of the children with their science projects for the science fair on Friday. It should be fun and interesting.

MARCH 15, 20—

I got a lot done today. I put up a bulletin board, watered the kids' lima beans, made a spelling Bingo game, and cut out positive reward incentives.

(Janet Joyce's log continues in this fashion, discussing how she helps the children make rabbit masks and helps to give an I.Q. test. She also discusses her concern about a child who threatens to run away and commit suicide, as well as her worries about how to discipline the children when they misbehave. She and the teacher-aide develop a management plan. She discusses getting ready to teach a social studies unit in which the children develop their own questions based on the table of contents of a chapter in their textbook.)

Assisting the Teacher

An important, early school-based step toward the teaching process is assisting the teacher in a variety of noninstructional classroom duties, which allows education students to apply some of what they have learned in their college classes and in-school observation without taking primary responsibility for students before they are ready.

First, the student participant and classroom teacher should discuss what type of assistance would be most helpful to the teacher and valuable to the class. There are hundreds of noninstructional duties in which teachers are involved every day. They include activities as diverse as taking attendance and placing student work on the bulletin board. Although most of these duties are routine tasks, they support the important work of teaching and learning. Classroom routines usually can be placed in one of these categories: physical condition of the room, movement of the children, handling materials and papers, keeping records and reports, classroom procedures, and special drills, classes, and days.

Many student participants incorrectly assume that such tasks are demeaning and prevent active participation in the classroom. On the contrary, these routines are essential to managing the classroom, and the teacher who does not master them is rarely able to teach. Initially, routine tasks assumed by the student participants should not directly involve the children. We have provided you with a checklist of some of these activities.

SAMPLE FORM 37

Checklist of Routines for Helping the Teacher

STUDENT: Reggie Gomez

TEACHER: Mr. Downs

GRADE LEVEL AND/OR SUBJECT: Sixth grade; science

continued

DATES: September 11, 20— to October 24, 20—

OBJECTIVE: To participate in noninstructional classroom duties

Instructions to Student Participant: All of the following duties are important to the management of the instructional environment. You will need to learn to complete these while simultaneously teaching the students and managing the class. To help you learn to do so efficiently, complete all tasks appropriate to your teaching situation and indicate the date each is accomplished. Please have the classroom teacher sign this form when all appropriate activities have been successfully completed.

Activity	Date Completed
1. Make a seating chart	September 11
2. Take attendance	September 16
3. Run errands for the classroom teacher	September 3
4. Help with classroom housekeeping	September 3
5. Organize materials needed for a lesson	September 26
6. Make copies of materials needed for the lesson	September 18
7. Help pass out materials to the students	September 4
8. Arrange a bulletin board	October 3
9. Check out books from the library to be used by students in the classroom	September 13
10. Check out media to be used in a lesson	October 14
11. Make a chart or graph	October 29
12. Make a transparency or stencil	September 16
13. Run a film, filmstrip, videotape, etc.	October 21
14. Get supplementary materials needed for a lesson (magazine illustrations, pamphlets, maps, etc.)	September 16
15. Develop a bibliography for an upcoming unit	November 4
16. Correct papers	September 19
17. Set up or help set up a lab	October 21
18. Write news/assignments on the chalkboard	October 5
19. Set up a learning center	November 18
20. Set up an experiment or a demonstration	October 24
21. Obtain a speaker to come to class, or help organize a class field trip	November 15
22. Help gather materials for a class party	November 22
23. Help make costumes for a class play	October 24
24. Send out a class newsletter to parents	did not do
25. Other (please list below):	October 26

Supervised playground, took children to bus.

I certify that the student participant listed above has successfully completed all of the above activities that are appropriate to my classroom.

Mr. Downs
_____
(Classroom teacher's signature)

After student participants work in classrooms for a few days and begin to learn the routine and know the children, they can broaden their activities to include those that directly involve the children. We provide you with a checklist of some of these activities in Sample Form 38.

SAMPLE FORM 38

Checklist of Routines Involving Students

STUDENT: Alex Gerstenberger

TEACHER: Mrs. Caudle

GRADE LEVEL AND/OR SUBJECT: Eighth grade; social studies

DATES: September 19, 20— to November 14, 20—

OBJECTIVE: To determine students' skills, motivation, and interests in a teaching/learning situation

Instructions to Student Participant: All of the following activities are important to the instruction of the students. You will need to learn to complete these while simultaneously teaching the students and managing the class. To help you learn to do so efficiently, complete all tasks appropriate to your teaching situation and indicate the date each is accomplished. Please have the classroom teacher sign this form when all appropriate activities have been successfully completed.

Activity	Date Completed
1. Orient a new student	September 19
2. Help individual students with seatwork	September 11
3. Work with a club or student activity	October 14
4. Assist a small group	September 24
5. Work with an individual student in a lab (i.e., computer, language, or science)	September 27
6. Assist a disabled student	October 18
7. Assist students with library research	October 31
8. Monitor a test	November 14
9. Collect money	September 6
10. Hand out and collect materials	September 6
11. Listen to an individual student read or recite a lesson	September 26
12. Give a test or a quiz	November 11
13. Assist young children with clothing	N/A
14. Bring books or materials to share with the students	October 15
15. Supervise students outside the classroom	October 21
16. Read aloud or tell a story	September 30
17. Help students in a learning center	November 6
18. Accompany students to a school office, the bus, or the playground	September 26
19. Attend a parent-teacher conference	October 29
20. Work with the teacher in developing an IEP (Individual Education Plan) for a mainstreamed student	November 8
21. Accompany students to before- or after-school programs	Daily beginning September 9
22. Help monitor the hallway, lunchroom, or playground	September 9
23. Other (please list below):	

Worked with small groups in computer lab for 30 minutes, two days a week.

I certify that the student participant listed above has successfully completed all of the above activities that are appropriate to my classroom.

Mrs. Caudle
(Classroom teacher's signature)

Preparing to Teach

Most uninitiated observers of the teaching process believe that teaching is lecturing to a large group of students. Many contend that anyone who has knowledge and can speak, can teach. These contentions are based on the assumption that the teacher must be perpetually on stage. Of course, this is only a small part of what a teacher does. In fact, many teachers rarely stand in front of a large group of children—and they may be excellent teachers.

Teaching involves employing many activities at once. In addition to the routine tasks described previously, classroom teachers frequently find themselves teaching small groups of students while they are instructing individuals within the group.

At the same time, they may be observing the activities of other students in the classroom. If a teacher, for example, knows that four students are at the math center, and that one of them is likely to have difficulty with the new word problem added today, he makes a mental note to see if the student needs help as soon as he finishes with another group. The teacher is also aware of the students working on a science experiment at the back sink, and he listens carefully for any sound that might indicate that playing with water is more interesting than using it in the experiment. The teacher hears beeps and burps from the computers, so he knows that the students are busily engaged. He is also aware that in fifteen minutes he must interrupt all of this activity so that there is time to introduce the children to the new social studies unit before lunch. When he hears a knock on the door he is not surprised; he knows that the door monitor will open it. Jacob Kounin describes the teacher's simultaneous involvement in dozens of activities as "withitness" (1970). Being able to focus on so many activities at once is not easy, nor does it come naturally to the beginner. "Withitness" is a skill learned from considerable experience with the variety of activities that occur in the classroom.

To help develop this essential skill, student participants should begin their teaching experiences with the smallest unit of classroom instruction—tutoring a single student in a single skill or concept. From here, they can proceed to working with a small group of students, initially using the classroom teacher's plan, as Janet Joyce does, and later using their own plans. After all of this has been successfully accomplished, they can tackle teaching a lesson to the entire class. At first, teaching might be done using the teacher's plan; afterward, with the help of the teacher, it might be done by developing more independent plans. After significant practice using all of these teaching skills, the student participant should begin developing "withitness."

Planning to Teach

Before any teaching is done, whether it be tutoring a single child or teaching a lesson to the entire class, planning is essential. Planning for anything—a social function, what college to attend, where to go on vacation—can be a difficult task. All planning requires reflecting on the past and anticipating the future. We recommend that preservice teachers practice their planned lessons prior to presenting them to students in the classroom. The consequences of failing to plan are usually more painful than the labor of planning. Thus, for the teacher, the consequences of an unplanned or poorly planned lesson may include embarrassment, preoccupation with discipline, loss of control, and a poor evaluation by a superior. Similarly, the student may also suffer such consequences as loss of interest, disruptive behavior, and limited or no learning. The anecdote that follows gives one teacher's account of a lesson with little or no planning.

"Running Account" of an Unplanned Lesson

AIM: To discuss digestion

PROCEDURE: A pupil will give a report that will lead to a class discussion

MATERIALS: Mimeographed drawing of the digestive process in hands of the pupils, and a sketch on the board of the same process.

Teacher	Pupils	Supervisory comment
	"Mr. Gale, the diagram on the board says it takes four days for digestion to take place. Isn't that wrong?"	
"The boy who copied it down for me made a mistake."	"But. Mr. Gale, the mimeographed sheet you gave us reads the same way."	Teacher loses respect by failing to admit his error.
"Well, then, it's wrong. It should be four hours. Let's forget that until I take the roll." (Calls off names one by one.)		Uneconomic use of time. Should have a seating chart.
"John, get up here and give your report."	(Report, obviously copied from an encyclopedia, is read in three minutes.)	Pupils are evidently not taught how to make or give a report.
"Is that all? Read it again."	"Do we have to take notes on this? Will we be tested on this?"	Indicates lack of any organized procedure.
"Certainly, everything we do here is important. Joan, you come to the board and take down important data in John's report."		Yet notebooks of pupils around me contain no science notes.
"John, read your report."	"I've read it twice." (Girl at board is not clear on what to do.)	Introduces a new procedure without preparing the class.
"We'll finish this tomorrow. Get out some paper. I'm going to give you a quiz. Copy down these questions."	(Class is very noisy.)	Teacher improvising. Had no alternative plan worked out.
"All right, not too much talking."		
"There is too much noise here. There is no need for it."		
"Now look! What is all this chattering about? Stop it."	"You didn't teach us any of this."	Quiz evidently not prepared beforehand.
"This is supposed to be a quiz. Would you mind moving apart a little?"	(Pupils unconcerned and talk throughout the quiz.)	Teacher's lack of planning and procedure is leading to chaos.
"Do you know what you can put down on this paper—zero."		

continued

Teacher	Pupils	Supervisory comment
"Look! I'm getting fed up. Come to detention this afternoon."		Threats ineffective. Class does not respect or fear teacher.
"Do you realize that you people cannot keep quiet for five minutes?"		
"All right. I'll collect the papers, and we will go into tomorrow's lesson."		Collects papers one by one.
"Anybody know what a spectrum is?"	"Something like a color wheel." (Aimless discussion for about ten minutes.)	Teacher improvising.
"Read this chapter for tomorrow."		Assignment nebulous.
"Quiet now! I am going to open the door to see if classes have been dismissed."		School has a bell system. Teacher cannot wait to escape from the noise.

Source: Thomas J. Brown. *Student Teaching in a Secondary School,* 1968.

When teaching, successful planning requires thorough knowledge of the content, an understanding of a variety of methods for presenting the content, and knowledge of the psychological readiness of the pupils. Any teacher who assumes that learning ends with the baccalaureate degree is not likely to be very successful. This was acknowledged when the Interstate New Teacher Assessment and Support Consortium (INTASC) developed standards recognizing that all teachers, at every career stage, must possess core knowledge and skills. As a teacher's career matures, his or her knowledge and skills must also become more sophisticated. Some subjects and skills that today's teachers teach were not a part of the curriculum when they attended school. For example, many teachers have had neither courses nor even instruction in computers, but they now must teach word processing, using the Internet, computer graphics, computer programming, and even computer ethics. Likewise, they use CD-ROM technology and PowerPoint presentations to teach their lessons. For some teachers, the information superhighway allows their students to communicate with students at universities around their state and even children in Japan. None of this was even a remote possibility during their years in school and in some cases even during their undergraduate, teacher-education programs. Likewise, the world of teacher education is continually developing and changing. Many classroom teachers did not focus on teaching standards, teaching styles, multiple intelligences, or multicultural education during their college careers. Today, knowledge of each of these areas and an ability to integrate the knowledge into the curriculum and teaching is critical. Therefore, one of the most important steps to success in planning to teach and in teaching is continous study.

Developing Plans

Although planning is always time consuming, it is not a difficult process. Planning is a skill involving a series of steps that can be taught and learned. Assuming the teacher has knowledge of both the content to be taught and the students, the steps in planning are as follows:

PREPLANNING

1. Examine the ten principles of teaching standards.

2. Consider the ability levels, learning styles, and multiple intelligences of the students.

3. Examine school district, county, or state curriculum guides.

4. Determine which goal(s) you will address in the lesson. (A goal is a learning end.)

5. Select the topic of the lesson.

6. Gather materials and examples. Be sure you have selected ones that are appropriate for the pupils (e.g., Do you need left-handed scissors? Can your kindergarten students do a print that requires multiple colors of paint in a single class session? Have you included materials that represent the ethnic, cultural, racial, and religious background of your students?).

7. Identify what students already know the topic.

8. Determine the duration of the lesson.

PLANNING

1. Write the goal(s) you plan to address at the top of your plan.

2. Develop specific, short-term objectives for your lesson. (Objectives are what you hope the pupils will accomplish by the end of the lesson.)

3. Select the materials you will use.

4. Identify an appropriate teaching methodology (or a variety of methodologies).

5. Arrange the materials and/or steps in a logical sequence. (Ask yourself: Is the amount of material and number of steps appropriate for the maturity of the students and length of the class period?)

6. Choose appropriate teaching activities and experiences.

7. Decide how learning will be assessed.

PRETEACHING

1. Prepare class handouts, audiovisuals, etc.

2. Review or preview any materials you will be using in the lesson. (Be sure that if students will be using materials individually you have previewed them as well.)

3. Review your plan.

The following plan was developed by a student participant who used the steps outlined above to meet a state literal comprehension goal for tenth graders. This student used the lesson plan format in Chapter Two, pp. 33, 34, 35, to design her lesson and meet the state goal: "The learner will identify [the] *sequence* of events." This and other lesson plan formats that can be used to design lessons can be found at the end of this book in Part V, Forms.

SAMPLE FORM 39

Lesson Plan Form 1

STUDENT: Juan Gomez

TEACHER: Mrs. Ricardo

GRADE LEVEL AND/OR SUBJECT: Tenth grade; English

DATE AND TIME: December 9, 20—, 8:30 a.m.

OBJECTIVE: To prepare a seven-step lesson plan to be used in teaching a specific lesson.

Instructions to the Student Participant: Whether your plan covers several classroom sessions or only one, each lesson should include an outline of your goal, objectives, materials, and expected lesson duration in addition to the seven steps listed below:

Goal: To teach the learner to identify sequence of events

Objectives:
1. The learners will identify the sequence of events in a videotape of a popular television show, "Murder She Wrote."

2. The learners will identify the sequence of events, using the format established by the class, in the short story, "Four and Twenty Blackbirds," by Agatha Christie.

Materials:
1. Videotape player and television.

2. The videotape of an episode of "Murder She Wrote."

3. Chalk.

4. Twenty-five copies of "Adventures in Appreciation," the literature text containing the Christie story.

5. Five sheets of newsprint, five magic markers, and masking tape.

6. Overhead projector, blank transparency, and marker pen.

Duration: Two sixty-minute class periods.

FIRST CLASS

1. **Anticipatory Set**
   Today we're going to be seeing a videotape of a recent episode of "Murder, She Wrote." (This alone will provide the motivation.)
   How many of you have seen that show on T.V.?
   Who is the main character on the show? (Jessica Fletcher, a mystery writer/ detective.)
   What usually happens in the show? (List responses on chalkboard—Be sure students determine the following: Murder usually occurs early in the show. During the remainder of the show, we are introduced to various suspects to learn their motives and alibis. Jessica spends her time researching such clues as the murder weapon. Throughout the show, we are presented with many "red herrings," which attempt to lead us to the wrong conclusion. By the end of the episode the murder is solved.)
   Write SAVE on the board; this information will be needed tomorrow. (5 minutes)

2. **Objective**
We will be looking for the exact sequence of events in today's episode. You'll need a notebook and a pen. Put everything else under your chairs. Write down each event as it occurs; you might want to use the outline on the board to assist you in the process. Remember, you are looking for the exact sequence of events. Be sure to take careful notes because you will need them in class tomorrow. (Wait for students to have notebook and pen on desk and everything else under their chairs.) (5 minutes)

3. **Teacher Input**
View the video of "Murder, She Wrote." (Watch video from rear of the room to monitor students' attention and notetaking.) (45 minutes)

SECOND CLASS

4. **Checking for Understanding**
Take out the notes you took yesterday on the "Murder, She Wrote" video. Put everything else under your chairs.
    Let's review the sequence we recorded on the board yesterday. (Call students' attention to SEQUENCE written on board.)
        Did you see a similar sequence in this episode? (5 minutes)
        Did you find any "red herrings"? (5 minutes)

5. **Guided Practice**
You will be outlining the specific events of this episode in your activity groups. (Note: This assumes students are assigned to long-term activity groups, and they know the procedure to be used in completing group-work.) The assignment for your group-work is written on the board.

ASSIGNMENT ON THE BOARD AS FOLLOWS:
Group-Work Assignment

1. Select a recorder.
2. List on the newsprint provided, the sequence of events in the episode of "Murder, She Wrote." Be sure to include all elements outlined on the board.
3. You have ten minutes to complete this task. When you have finished, post your newsprint on the side wall, using the masking tape provided.
    (While students are working in groups, place a copy of the literature anthology under each chair.)
    After groups have completed their sequence-of-events charts, compare each sequence chart with the class. On the overhead projector, create a class sequence of events. Discuss why some groups sequenced the events of the story differently. (25 minutes)

6. **Independent Practice**
Now we will independently read Agatha Christie's "Four and Twenty Blackbirds," found in your literature anthology on page 16.
    Have any of you heard of Agatha Christie before? Have you read anything by her? (She is a famous British mystery writer, known particularly for her murder mysteries. The detective in this story is one of her two famous detectives, Hercule Poirot, who is always investigating cases in London. (Note: The other famous detective is Miss Marple.)
    As you read this story, outline the sequence of events just as we did for "Murder, She Wrote." I'll leave the original outline of the sequence of events we did yesterday on the board to help you. I'll also leave the one we just completed on the overhead to help

continued

you. You'll need to do this in your notebook. We'll have about 20 minutes to read today in class. If you do not finish the story, you'll need to finish it for homework. I will be collecting the sequence you do for this story tomorrow at the beginning of class. (This will be used to assess the students' understanding of the sequence-of-events concept as well as their understanding of Christie's story.) Any questions? (As students are reading, put homework assignment on the board.)

ASSIGNMENT ON THE BOARD AS FOLLOWS:
Homework Assignment

1. Finish reading "Four and Twenty Blackbirds" by Agatha Christie ("Adventures in Appreciation," pages 16–25).
2. On notebook paper, list the sequence of events of the story.
3. The assignment will be collected tomorrow at the beginning of class. (25 minutes)

7. **Closure**
Five minutes before the end of the class, ask the students to stop reading and pay attention to a brief discussion.
Summarizing questions to involve the students in synthesizing the lesson:
—How was this story similar to the episode of "Murder, She Wrote?"
—Did the sequence follow the model we put on the board?
—How did the story differ from the episode of "Murder, She Wrote?"
—Did Christie present you with any "red herrings"?
—Your assignment for tomorrow is on the board.

Source: Lois Sprinthall. *A Strategy Guide for Teachers: Guidebook for Supervisors of Novice Teachers.* Unpublished manuscript. Based on the work of Madeline Hunter.

Because there are so many different formats you can use in planning lessons, we have included an additional one below. You, your school-based cooperating teacher, or your university supervisor can select any one of these formats, or you might want to try both of these to see which one works best for you. It is also likely that your cooperating teacher or university supervisor has another format he or she would like you to try. It doesn't matter which lesson plan format you use as long as it gives you all the information you need to teach and evaluate your lesson effectively. Likewise, it is also important that the lesson plan format you select makes articulation between other lessons within a unit or across subject areas easy to accomplish. A lesson should not stand alone, but rather be a part of an entire curriculum.

SAMPLE FORM 40

Lesson Plan Form 2

STUDENT: Stephanie Price

TEACHER: Mrs. Lauringburg

GRADE LEVEL AND/OR SUBJECT: Eighth grade; language arts/social studies

TOPIC: Geographic study of the arctic region

DATE AND TIME: December 4, 20—, 11:15 a.m.

Instructions to the Student Participant: Whether your plan covers several classroom sessions or only one, each lesson should include an outline of your objectives, procedures, materials, and evaluation.

Objectives: Students will be able to:
> Respond to the warmup writing prompt.
> Locate the Arctic region on a world map and a globe and relate that location to their home on map/globe.
> Define ten unusual words used to describe the Arctic region.
> Use the Internet to learn more about the Arctic.

Procedures: Warmup writing/discussion activity
> Students identify where the Arctic region is in relation to their home and make assumptions about climate based on relationship to the equator.
> PowerPoint presentation with discussion throughout.
> Students will identify ten works during the presentation that are unusual to them and define the words.
> After the presentation, students will do Internet activity, work on vocabulary, and answer essay-response question.
> The work is due at the end of class.

Materials: Computers, Averkey, map, globe

Website: Arctic Study Center Web—http://www.mnh.si.edu/arctic/html/weblinks

Evaluation: Students will turn in completed work: vocabulary, short-essay responses, and answers to the following:
> What two new things did you learn from the link?
> What is the most surprising or interesting thing you learned from the link?
> Did the link just reinforce what you have learned so far about the Arctic region or was there something discussed which makes you want to find out more about the Arctic?
> Would you recommend this site to a friend? Why or why not?

Source: Stephanie Price, Student, University of North Carolina at Asheville. Unpublished.

The student participant, Juan Gomez, who taught the lesson in a tenth-grade English class (Sample Form 39) understood, after reflecting on it with the classroom teacher, that it would lead to several more complex lessons. A unit (a series of lessons addressing a single topic) on mystery writing was planned for several weeks later, and the lesson described in this chapter was used as an advance organizer for the unit to help students understand the plotting techniques used by mystery writers. During the unit, the tenth graders would also write their own narratives, learning to employ sequencing techniques. Likewise, they would examine plot sequence in a variety of other literary genres, including fantasy, historical fiction, and adventure/suspense.

Sequencing lessons in an entire program is a very important part of teaching. Therefore, it is necessary for student participants to examine curriculum guides designed by the district, county, or state (as discussed in Chapter Three) so that they can begin to understand how their lessons fit into the entire curriculum. Likewise, it is essential that student participants work with classroom teachers to develop lesson plans, so that the teacher can help them understand this sequence of objectives, goals, lessons, and units. A unit plan format (41A) is provided at the end of this book in Part V, Forms. A sample unit plan is presented below.

SAMPLE FORM 41

Unit Plan Format

STUDENT: Emily Jowdy

TEACHER: Mr. Barnes

GRADE LEVEL AND/OR SUBJECT: Twelfth grade; government and economics

DATE: January 16, 20—

UNIT: The Ties That Bind

DURATION: Eight to ten weeks

OBJECTIVE: To plan a series of related, sequential lesson plans on a particular theme to be taught over an extended period of time.

Overview: Many times our students take back-to-back courses in government and economics. In order to show them that these concepts are interrelated and constantly changing, a unit can be planned over an extended period.

Purpose: One purpose of this activity is to expand the understanding of students in the areas of both economics and government. Another purpose is to show the relationship between these two subjects and how, over the course of time, our views regarding the two subjects have changed. The third purpose is to show the relationship of these ideas to current political and economic issues.

Objectives: Students will be able to:

1. Explain and present to their classmates the concepts presented by economists since the time of Adam Smith, put these concepts into historical perspective and, where applicable, relate these ideas to current issues.

2. Understand that both political and economic systems are ever-changing and that a change in either one of these systems may cause a change in the other.

3. Sort out those economists who have contributed lasting achievements in their field from those who may have been of only passing importance or a novelty of their times.

Activities: Over the course of the unit, the students will be divided into five groups and will be asked to give a presentation. Each of the groups will be provided with a list of both general requirements and specific requirements for their selected/assigned economist(s).

At the assigned time, each group will present its project to the class. The following requirements must be included in each of these reports:

1. The report must be oral.

2. There must be some type of visual aid to accompany the presentation.

3. The report must be documented with five to ten sources, including the Internet.

4. The report must have originality and creativity—just reading a report is not acceptable.

After the report has been presented, the class has the opportunity to ask questions of the presenters concerning any material that was not clearly explained.

Resources/Materials Needed:

Folbre, N. 1995. *The New Field Guide to the U.S. Economy: A Compact and Irreverent Guide to Economic Life in America.* New York: New Press.

Heilbroner, Robert. L. 1999. *The Worldly Philosopher.* New York: Touchstone Books.

Johnson P. 1998. *A History of the American People.* New York: Harper Collins.

Sante Fe Institute Studies in the Sciences of Complexity. 1997. *The Economy as a Revolving Complex System.* Eds D. A. Lane, W. B. Arthur, S. N. Durlauf. New York: Longman.

Internet; Visual aids

Tying It All Together:

Evaluation: At the end of each of the presentations, all of the students are given a written test of the material. Those students who are responsible for the presentation are also given a grade for it.

General Comments: Over the course of the unit, as the ideas of the various economists are studied, students are (through directed questions) led to an understanding of how the ideas about both government and economics have changed and how interrelated these two subjects are. This is a difficult concept for some students to understand, but one that is necessary if students are to truly understand the basis for our government and economic systems and why we, as a nation, are constantly re-evaluating and refining them.

Source: Adapted from http://ofcn.org/cyber.serv/academy/acc/soc/cecsst/cecsstio.num OFCNS Academy Curricular Exchange—Social Studies. Mary J. Williams. Monroe Catholic High School, Fairbanks, AK, 1997.

SAMPLE FORM 42

Reflective Observation of Preteaching and Planning

NAME OF OBSERVER: Richard Blackburn

DATE AND TIME OF REFLECTIVE OBSERVATION: May 22, 20—, 1:15 p.m.

TEACHER/SCHOOL: Mr. Romano Ellenboro Elementary

GRADE LEVEL AND/OR SUBJECT: Fifth grade

OBJECTIVE OF OBSERVATION: To think carefully and reflect about your participation, preteaching, and planning. Below are some guiding questions/statements related to each of the five steps in the reflection cycle (Chapter One, pp. 9, 10, 11). The questions/statements are directly related to the ten principles from the INTASC Standards (Chapter Two, pp. 37, 38, 39).

Instructions to the Observer: Respond to the following questions on Form 42A after you have completed participation, preteaching, and planning.

1. **Select**
   a. What preteaching activities did you complete?
   b. What kind of planning did you do before your teaching?
   c. What principles from INTASC Standards did you address?

continued

2. **Describe**
   a. List the steps you used in the planning process.
   b. Describe the parts of your lesson plan.
   c. Describe the parts of your unit plan.

3. **Analyze**
   a. If you have utilized more than one lesson planning format, which was more successful? Why?
   b. How do you relate planning a lesson to teaching a lesson?
   c. How did your preteaching and planning prepare you for your future teaching?
   d. Which preteaching activities were most helpful to you?

4. **Appraise**
   a. What planning techniques were most helpful to you?
   b. How effective were you in checking classroom routines?
   c. How effective were you in checking students' routines?

5. **Transform**
   a. What lesson and/or unit planning techniques will you use in your future teaching? Why?
   b. What additional planning skills would you like to develop?
   c. What did you learn about planning for using the Internet that you can use in your classroom teaching?

Source: Adapted from North Carolina State Department of Public Instruction. *Performance Based Licensure*, Raleigh, NC, 1998–1999.

⑥ Chapter Six
Teaching

Initial Teaching Experiences

Your initial teaching experiences should be successful ones. To ensure their success, you should plan carefully and begin slowly. A good place to begin is working with a single student. The first session should be devoted to getting to know the student and letting the student get to know you. Your objective for that session might be simply, "The learner will discuss something about himself or herself with the tutor."

Most student participants are nervous when they face a student or a class for the first time. These jitters are normal, but once you get started, the plan you have developed should give you increasing confidence. To ensure that your plan will be successful, discuss it with the classroom teacher prior to implementing it.

Try to begin each new teaching experience with something you enjoy. For example, you might spend an early session reading and discussing a story you love. Or, you might do part of a lesson in which you discuss a trip you took. If the fifth-grade social studies class is studying Mexico and you recently visited Mexico, your first short lesson plan might include some Mexican music, a few slides you took, sharing a Mexican story, discussing Mexican food, etc.

In order for you to develop your teaching skills, it is essential that you increase your understanding of teaching standards, learn to reflect on your actual teaching experiences, and share these reflections with classroom cooperating teachers and college or university supervisors. As you work through this chapter, we advise you to review the reflective process described in Chapter One, pp. 9, 10, 11, and the ten performance-based teaching principles outlined in Chapter Two, pp. 37, 38, 39.

The Importance of Teaching Standards

Just as it is important to set high standards for our students in order to encourage learning, it is critical that we have high standards for ourselves as teachers. You were introduced to the concept of standards in Chapter Two. You have used the standards established by the Interstate New Teacher Assessment and Support Consortium (INTASC) in the reflections you have completed. It is our hope that your understanding of the standards and their importance to your growth as a teacher will deepen as you work through the forms in this chapter.

According to researcher Linda Darling-Hammond, the INTASC standards hold promise for mobilizing reforms in the teaching profession—reforms that will lead to higher-quality teaching. In addition, the standards will help structure the learning process of preservice and inservice teachers by articulating the complex nature of teaching through the ten performance-based principles. These principles capture the interactive nature of teaching. In addition, the common core standards acknowledge that teachers must grow and develop throughout their careers. Therefore, the forms suggested for use by preservice teachers could continue to be used throughout the teacher's career.

Researchers have found that using the INTASC standards during preservice observation and teaching helps teacher-education students gradually integrate them into their practice. Likewise, the more they are used to reflect on what has been observed, planned for, and taught, the more likely preservice teachers are to develop awareness of and appreciation for them. This leads to principled decision making and an ability to plan approaches to or make changes in their own teaching (Bliss and Mazur 1997). This, then, is what we hope for you.

Tutoring

Tutoring, teaching, or guiding—usually an individual child—is a very important function of the classroom teacher. Unfortunately, little time is available in most large, public-school classrooms to work with students one to one. Therefore, the student participants who act as tutors are not only developing teaching skills, but are also providing an important service for the classroom teacher and the students they are tutoring.

Types of Tutoring

Two major types of tutoring are (1) short-term and informal, and (2) long-term and planned. Student participants can experience the first kind of tutoring while assisting the teacher. For example, while pupils work on individual projects, the student participants might be wandering around the classroom, bending down to the eye level of the children, reading their stories, making comments, and asking questions. This is informal, short-term tutoring. The kind we will emphasize in this chapter, however, requires planning.

Tutoring that requires planning includes teaching skills in language, mathematics, social studies, science, computers, art, music, health, physical education, etc. Usually, though not always, this type of tutoring is done with pupils who are experiencing difficulty learning the skill or have missed learning class skills due to absence.

Tutoring may also involve diagnosing specific strengths and weaknesses. For example, as the pupil reads aloud to the tutor, the tutor might be looking for specific reading problems. Sometimes tutoring is used to remedy these weaknesses. A kindergarten teacher might notice that one student is unable to hold his scissors and cut a simple outline. The teacher has noticed other problems in this child's motor skills when the child is doing physical activities. Since the teacher suspects problems in eye-hand coordination, the tutor will select activities to help the child develop these skills.

Sometimes tutoring is used to give certain students individual attention. For example, a student may be experiencing home problems or may have a special talent that is not encouraged during the regular class. He or she may be disabled, or the teacher may simply feel the child has been neglected because so many other pupils require special attention. To help you determine the tutoring activities in which *you* can be involved, a checklist is provided on the next page.

SAMPLE FORM 43

Checklist of Tutoring Activities

STUDENT: Nicholas Rapparlie

NAME OF PUPIL(S) TUTORED (IF APPROPRIATE): Frank Mozolic

TEACHER: Mr. Sulinski

GRADE LEVEL AND/OR SUBJECT: Fourth grade; reading/language arts/math

DATES: September 6, 20— to October 30, 20—

OBJECTIVE: To develop teaching skills and to determine students' interests

Instructions to Student Participant: Listed below and on the following pages are several types of short-term and long-term tutoring activities in which you can participate. As you complete these activities, indicate the date each is accomplished. At the end of each section there is space for your comments about what you learned from the tutoring activities. Please have the classroom teacher sign this form when your activities have been completed.

Short-Term, Informal Tutoring Activities	Date Completed
1. Ask individual students questions about something they are reading or writing, a picture they are drawing, or a project they are working on.	September 17
2. Discuss with individual students, stories they have read.	September 19
3. Help students with their seatwork.	September 6
4. Answer questions students have about their individual work.	September 23

Comment on what you learned from these activities:

I learned that fourth graders seem to forget a lot over the summer. Some needed help with easy words like "master," and some needed help with simple multiplication. Many liked to draw about outer space and tell me about their Nintendo games. A few liked to read stories about racing cars and Antarctica.

Long-Term, Planned Tutoring Activities	Date Completed
1. Teaching skills that have not been mastered by individual students (grammar, composition, reading, mathematical computations, times tables, word problems, word processing, using a computer program, using a table of contents, reading a textbook for meaning, cutting out objects, using a microscope, etc.). List the skill(s) you taught:	October 22

Syllabication—dividing between two syllables; after prefixes and before suffixes

	Date Completed
2. Diagnosing a student's strength or weakness (administering a specific individual test, listening to a student read, asking a student questions on a variety of levels, watching a student do a mathematical computation, observing a student using a computer program, watching a student use a piece of equipment, etc.). List the method(s) you employed and what you were attempting to diagnose:	September 27

Had student read six passages from grade levels 1–6 silently; then had student respond to five questions of varied levels of difficulty after each passage. I wanted to determine the student's comprehension level. It was fifth grade.

continued

Long-Term, Planned Tutoring Activities	Date Completed

3. Remedying a weakness (helping a student learn to cut out a shape with scissors, assisting a student with rules of phonics or grammar, drilling a student on vocabulary, showing a student how to find meaning in a paragraph, demonstrating for a student how to use a piece of equipment safely, etc.). List the method(s) you employed and the weakness you were attempting to remedy:

October 30

—Listed Halloween words for student to divide into syllables and use those words to write a Halloween story.

—Wanted to determine if student could apply syllabication rules.

4. Developing a special talent (teaching the student a technique of drawing, reading a piece of student writing and providing support and suggestions, listening to a student read and discussing what has been read, talking to a student about a historical event, working with a student on a science project, helping a student complete a woodworking project, teaching basic computer programming, taking the student to a museum, etc.). List the method(s) you employed and the talent you were attempting to develop:

September 11

Wanted to motivate student to read about current events from newspapers/journals, not just hear them on TV. We read reports of The Los Alomos Fire, hoping this would motivate him to read further.

5. Other. List specific long-range tutoring activities in which you have participated:

October 17

Helped student do research on controlled burning in national parks. Student needed a lot of help finding and using a variety of reference/media material. He did write a good outline and a fairly good paper.

Comment on what you learned from these activities:

Students at this age need to practice library skills and use them in their writing.

I certify that the student participant listed above has successfully completed those tutoring activities indicated above.

Mr. Sulinski

(Classroom teacher's signature)

Planning for Tutoring

To ensure that tutoring is as valuable as possible to the tutor as well as to the pupil, it is essential that careful planning is done prior to every session. The student participant should discuss with the classroom teacher the specific goals for the tutoring sessions. Then the tutor should check the INTASC standards and the ten performance-based principles. Next, the tutor should examine district, county, or state curriculum guides to determine where these goals fit in with the sequence of goals to be accomplished during the school year. Finally, the tutor should set specific objectives for each tutoring session.

For example, if the teacher's goal is to provide a child with more practice in reading aloud, the tutor checks the state curriculum guide and finds the following related goals: The learner will (1) demonstrate adequacy of *oral expression*, (2) demonstrate adequacy of *auditory discrimination* and *memory*, (3) develop *oral vocabulary*, and (4) demonstrate adequate *comprehension skill*. Likewise, the tutor discovers many goals in the areas of phonics and comprehension that might relate to the pupil's oral reading. In addition to these goals, the tutor examines INTASC standards related to diversity of learners, multiple instruction strategies, motivation, and management.

The tutor decides to begin with those goals directly related to reading aloud. Therefore, after a well-planned introductory session in which the tutor and pupil talk about themselves, the tutor begins the next session by asking the pupil to pick one of three stories she would like the tutor to read to her. The tutor has made sure that each of the stories relates to the unique characteristics of the child. Her selection might tell the tutor some things about the child with whom he is working. The tutor reads the story to her, stopping at appropriate points to discuss it. After they have completed the story, the tutor asks several questions about it, mentally noting areas of weakness in aural (listening) comprehension. Next, the tutor asks the pupil to read the story to him. He hopes that she will find this less threatening than reading a new story, since the story is already familiar to her. As the child reads, the tutor looks for specific problems she is experiencing. Immediately following the session, the tutor makes a list of these problems, discusses them with the classroom teacher, and uses them as the basis for some subsequent sessions. Finally, the tutor reflects on what has been accomplished and notes that in future sessions he will ask the child to do some art activities related to the story they are reading. What follows is a checklist you can use as you plan for tutoring.

SAMPLE FORM 44

Checklist for Planning a Tutorial

STUDENT: Robert Jones

NAME OF PUPIL(S) TUTORED: Billy Fields

GRADE LEVEL AND/OR SUBJECT: Fourth grade

DATES: September 26, 20— to October 20, 20—

OBJECTIVE: To develop teaching skills: diagnosing, planning, finding materials, conferencing, evaluating with the teacher

Instructions to Tutor: As you complete each of the following in your tutoring plans indicate the date completed.

Planning Activity	Date Completed
1. Discuss the student you will tutor with the classroom teacher.	September 26
2. Discuss possible tutoring topics and techniques with the classroom teacher.	September 26
3. Carefully plan an initial "getting-to-know-you" session with the student.	September 27
4. Diagnose student strengths and weaknesses as necessary.	September 30
5. Check INTASC standards and performance-based principles.	October 2
6. Check available curriculum guides to determine skills to be taught and their sequence.	October 3/4
7. Set a specific objective for each tutoring session.	October 7
8. Develop a plan for each tutoring session (appropriate plan formats can be found in Chapter Five pp. 33, 34, 35).	October 7 to October 15
9. Develop strategies that utilize your knowledge of multiple intelligences.	October 16
10. Consult appropriate resources for teaching techniques and materials.	October 17

continued

Planning Activity	Date Completed
11. Make sure all necessary materials are available and copied prior to each tutoring session.	October 18
12. Monitor the pupil's progress by keeping a log of each day's tutoring.	October 19
13. Discuss student's progress with the classroom teacher. Ask for additional suggestions for helping the student.	October 20

The basic elements of a tutoring lesson are the same as the elements of a lesson taught to a class. The tutor must:

1. Get the attention and interest of the pupil.

2. Relate the objective for the session.

3. Attempt to determine prerequisite learning, ask questions, and fill in gaps.

4. Guide the student through what is expected and model the learning to be accomplished.

5. Allow the student to attempt the skill/concept on his/her own.

6. Provide feedback.

7. Tie together the lesson by discussing what has been learned, what the pupil needs to do next, and what will be done in the next tutoring session. In addition, each session should provide some means of assessing the pupil's progress.

These steps are roughly parallel to the steps in a lesson plan (see Chapter Five, pp. 33, 34, 35) for an entire class and can be used, with limited modifications, for any type of tutoring. Following the tutoring the you should reflect on the session using the form supplied below.

SAMPLE FORM 45

Reflections on Tutoring Activities

NAME OF TUTOR: Richard Karpinski

DATE AND TIME OF RECORD: April 26, 20—, 10:50 a.m.

TEACHER/SCHOOL/GRADE: Mrs. Strablow, Miller Middle School, Seventh grade

OBJECTIVE OF OBSERVATION: To think carefully and reflect about your tutoring activities. Below are some guiding questions/statements which you can use for your reflection.

Instructions: Use Form 45A to respond to the questions after you have completed your tutoring.

1. **Select**
   a. What kind(s) of tutoring activities did you complete?
   b. Why did you decide to do the kind(s) of tutoring you did?
   c. How did the tutoring activities relate to the student(s) age(s)?
   d. What performance-based standard(s) (the ten principles) did you address?

2. **Describe**
   a. Briefly describe the pupil you tutored (age, gender, background, etc.).
   b. What special needs/interests did you consider when you planned the tutoring activity(ies)?
   c. What resources did you use?
   d. How did you monitor student progress?

3. **Analyze**
   a. How did your preplanning with the classroom teacher help you in planning for your tutoring sessions?
   b. How did the characteristics of the student affect your planning and tutoring?
   c. Did your tutoring plan allow for modification due to unanticipated student input? How?
   d. Why did you select the teaching strategies you incorporated in your lesson?

4. **Appraise**
   a. How different/similar were your objectives for each tutoring session?
   b. How effective were you in using available resources for your tutoring?

5. **Transform**
   a. What did you learn about planning for tutoring?
   b. How did you adjust your teaching as a result of student assessment?

Source: Adapted from North Carolina State Department of Public Instruction. *Performance Based Licensure*, Raleigh, NC, 1998–1999.

Small Groups

After student participants have worked successfully with one student in a tutoring situation, they may direct their teaching to a small group of students. Frequently, small groups of students work together without direct instruction to complete a task. However, the small group we will emphasize is a small instructional group, similar in many respects to the tutorial-teaching situation discussed previously. In fact, small-group instruction is frequently called multi-student tutoring.

Purposes of Small Groups

Penny Ur in her book, *Discussions That Work* (1981), points out many of the advantages of small-group work. One of the major advantages is increased participation by the students. In a classroom of thirty students, each individual can respond for a maximum of one minute during a thirty-minute lesson, and this assumes that the entire lesson involves student response. By contrast, in a group of five students each individual can respond for six minutes during the same thirty-minute period. Moreover, according to Ur, this heightened participation not only includes those who are articulate and frequently participate, but also those who are shy and rarely say anything in front of the class.

Second, according to Ur, the motivation of participants improves as they work in small groups. This is partly due to reduced inhibition, but it also occurs because group-work frequently focuses on individuals within the group, whereas whole-class work rarely focuses on individuals. The small group is more personal and participants are therefore more likely to want to be involved.

Small-group work lends itself to more active learning such as games, activities, learning centers, experiments, simulations, discussions, etc. Group-work, according to Ur, tends to be task-centered, and since students retain more from active rather than receptive instruction, small groups are likely to encourage more learning.

Group-work can free the teacher from the roles of instructor and controller. When students are working in small groups the teacher can move about the room, helping students when necessary and focusing attention on those who are most in need of assistance.

Group-work can allow for peer teaching, making both teaching and learning that occur in the classroom far more efficient than in the large-group situation. For example, if all students play the role of teacher as well as learner, the total amount of classroom teaching time is significantly increased. In addition, there is more variety in teaching techniques when more than one "teacher" instructs.

The National Assessment of Educational Progress (NAEP) analyzed third-, eighth-, and twelfth-grade students' responses to survey items about teaching methods used by their teachers. Then they compared them to the test results of the students. They concluded that students who work on mathematics problems in small groups using concrete materials achieve at a higher level on national standardized tests than those who simply watch the teacher work problems on the chalkboard (1990, 64). Likewise, according to NAEP, students who conduct science experiments with other students in small groups and then complete lab reports on the experiments or give oral reports have higher achievement test scores than those who observe teacher demonstrations or listen to teacher lectures. Similar results were found in comparing students' responses to survey items and achievement in history and civics. Students who work in small groups in which they do such things as complete map-work or write reports together score higher on the tests than students who merely read from a textbook and answer questions.

Additionally, small-group work provides a planned structure for implementing democratic education without permissiveness, according to Shlomo Sharan and Yaci Sharan in *Small Group Teaching* (1976). Student members of small groups are frequently involved in the decision-making process. They might select from several possible activities or various approaches to a single problem. Likewise, student members of groups select peers to take leadership roles. Elizabeth G. Cohen points out in *Designing Groupwork* that these types of activities transfer into adult work situations. Students interact in small groups much as adults must interact in work by asking questions, explaining, making suggestions, criticizing, listening, agreeing, disagreeing, and making joint decisions (1994, 3, 6).

James Moffett and Betty Jane Wagner in *Student-Centered Language Arts and Reading* (1992) contend that one of the most important reasons for small-group work is that it allows students to communicate with one another, which is important in developing language skills. Group-work allows for constructive classroom student talk. Allan C. Ornstein in his book, *Strategies for Effective Teaching* (1990), says that small-group work also has the advantage of enhancing student cooperation and social skills as well as providing an environment in which students can progress at their own pace. Utilizing small-group work is especially important with special-needs students, students with limited English, and students with low self-esteem. Chance, Morris, and Rakes state that "beginning preservice teachers can experience success with whole-class instruction while interacting with small groups and individual children" (1996, 387).

Functions of Small Groups

Small groups can have a variety of functions. They can facilitate learning by allowing students to work together on a skill that all members are having difficulty mastering. Each group might be assigned to read a different story or book. For example, all students who are reading one to two years below grade level may be grouped together for that subject. Individual groups may be working on an assigned or chosen research project, depending on their abilities or interests.

They can complete laboratory experiments and lab reports, or they can work on homework assignments during the last several minutes of a class period so that all students get a good start and know how to complete the assignments. Likewise, students can serve as an audience for their own writing in "writing circles", where they work together to help each other improve skills. They can practice dramatic performances in small groups or complete bulletin boards on interesting topics or themes in social studies, science, or English.

Brainstorming and/or discussion may be the objective of a small group in order to develop creativity or rational thinking skills. A group may work on a simulation game or in a play area in a preschool or elementary-school classroom. A group may be randomly assigned to complete a specified activity or to serve a management or class-government function. For example, students may plan a class trip or clean up the playground. Or, the group may be long term with students helping each other with specific skills such as writing or understanding fractions. In short, small-group teaching allows teachers to respond to diverse student needs, interests, abilities, intelligences, and backgrounds.

Structures of Small Groups

According to Alan Ornstein (1990), groups function best when they have from five to eight students. With fewer, the students tend to pair off rather than interact within the group. Other educators suggest that younger children tend to perform better in even smaller groups.

Frequently, first and second graders work better in pairs or in trios. However, the more experience the learners gain in group-work, the larger the group they can work in effectively. The student population included within the group will depend on the particular function of the group. As a general rule, Ornstein suggests that groups should be racially and ethnically mixed. Likewise, most groups function better if they have both male and female members. Finally, it is a good idea for preservice teachers to take into account behavior problems when forming groups, particularly those that will function independently. In most groups, the preservice teacher should mix ability and skill levels. It is not a good idea to formulate groups randomly or by "counting off". On the contrary, creating a group that will function effectively requires good preplanning. The sociogram (Sample Form 31, pp. 78, 79, 80) is a particularly useful tool to use prior to planning student groups.

The structure of any group varies according to its function. Frequently, small groups involve students working independently of the teacher on a project or problem arising from classroom work. At other times, groups may work with the teacher for a short period of time while the task or assignment is explained or guidance is given, and then work independently. Or the teacher may instruct one small group while other students in the class work without the teacher's direct guidance. In order to provide preservice teachers experience working with small classroom groups, we will focus on teacher-led groups in this chapter. Preservice teachers will want to include independent small groups in units and lessons planned and taught to the entire class.

Small-Group Instruction

Since classroom teachers frequently recognize a need to instruct small groups of students but have only limited time to do so, preservice teachers can meet an instructional need by assuming the responsibility for one small group. In an instructional group, the teacher's guidance is required to assist students in completing their task. Therefore, the small-group instruction designed by the student participant should be work that the students are unlikely to be able to complete successfully without instruction. This would include such things as skills they are having difficulty developing, new topics, introduction of new skills, and discussion of difficult topics or stories in order to bring learners to higher levels of cognition.

Planning for Small-Group Teaching

The sequence of the lesson plan is nearly the same as that for tutoring, but in this case several students are involved in the learning. Therefore, the preservice teacher must consider the needs and abilities of all group members to develop assessment instruments that can measure the progress of several students simultaneously.

SAMPLE FORM 46

Preplanning Small-Group Checklist

STUDENT: Kim Andrews

TEACHER: Shirley Walrod

GRADE LEVEL AND/OR SUBJECT: Eighth grade; science

DATES: November 3, 20— to November 12, 20—

OBJECTIVE: To practice my planning skills for small group instruction

Instructions to Student Participant: As you complete each of the following in planning for your small group, indicate the date completed.

Preplanning Activity	Date Completed
1. Discuss possible types of small-group teaching with the classroom teacher.	Novermber 3
2. Discuss the assignment of students to the small group.	November 3
3. Discuss the classroom teacher's goal for the small group.	November 3
4. Consider the needs, interests, abilities, and intelligences of the students who will participate in the instructional group. Discuss these issues with the classroom teacher.	November 5
5. Develop an assessment tool or technique that can measure the progress of several students simultaneously. (e.g., Students complete mathematics problems that begin slightly below their level of achievement and continue beyond their level of achievement. Students answer questions about reading samples that are below their reading level and continue beyond their reading level. Students complete multiple-choice items on a leveled vocabulary list. Students attempt to perform part of a one-act play. Students read parts orally in a short play, etc.)	November 6
6. Determine a specific objective for each small-group session.	November 7/8
7. Determine which of the behavior-based principles can be addressed in the small-group lesson.	November 9
8. Develop a plan for each small-group session. (Appropriate plan formats can be found in Chapter Five, pp. 33, 34, 35.)	November 9
9. Consult appropriate resources for teaching techniques and materials.	November 11

Preplanning Activity	Date Completed
10. Make sure all necessary materials are available and copied prior to each small-group session.	November 11
11. Monitor the pupils' progress by having them complete individual practice exercises related to each session's objective.	November 3 to November 11
12. Discuss the students' progress with the classroom teacher. Ask for additional suggestions for helping the students.	November 12

The student participant must be sure that all students in the group possess prerequisite knowledge for learning the concepts or skills to be taught. For example, if the students are grouped together to find the least common denominator, each student must already possess the prerequisite concepts of numerator, denominator, factor, and multiple, as well as know how to multiply and divide small whole numbers and how to add fractions with identical denominators. Therefore, an important part of planning for small-group instruction is determining each student's level of prerequisite knowledge.

To determine if students possess prerequisite skills and knowledge, you might want to begin the lesson, after you have gained the students' attention and explained the objective of the group-work, with a task you are sure they can accomplish. For example, the small group has been assigned to complete research on the Civil War from the perspective of various groups of Southerners (i.e., plantation owners, small planters, merchants, government officials, slaves). In order to accomplish this task, students will need to possess some basic research skills. Therefore, you decide to teach the lesson in the library. Early in the lesson, each student is required to find a reference book or article in a maximum of five minutes. If one or more of the students have problems finding the reference materials, you and the group members might discuss the problem. If most of the members seem unable to accomplish the task, you might decide to either teach library skills or obtain for them the reference material needed to complete the research. If the classroom teacher's goal is for the group to complete the research within a short period of time, the student participant, with the help of the librarian, might locate the materials for the students and then report to the classroom teacher the students' apparent weakness in library skills. A checklist of activities for small-group lessons follows.

SAMPLE FORM 47

Small-Group Teaching Checklist

STUDENT: Loretta Connor

TEACHER: Mr. Lebowitz

GRADE LEVEL AND/OR SUBJECT: Ninth grade; history

TOPIC: The Constitution

DATE AND TIME: November 20, 20—, 10:15 a.m.

OBJECTIVE: To implement a well-planned lesson and practice teaching skills

continued

Instructions to Student Participant: Use this checklist while planning and teaching your small group. To be sure that your lesson includes each of the following, check [✓] each item off as it occurs.

Teaching Activity	Appears in Lesson
1. The students' attention is grabbed.	✓
2. The objective of the lesson is related to the students.	✓
3. Prerequisite knowledge is ascertained through questions and answers, a quiz, completion of an exercise, etc.	✓
4. If appropriate, gaps in needed information are filled in.	✓
5. New information, skills, or materials are presented through explanation, demonstration, discussion, etc.	✓
6. Individual tasks are assigned to each group member.	n/a
7. Student performance is elicited and monitored through independent work.	✓
8. Teacher feedback is provided to each student.	✓
9. Student work is related to previous and future learning.	✓
10. Students review what they have learned in the lesson.	✓
11. The objective for the next small-group lesson is determined and communicated to the students.	✓

Although the small-group instructor must remain flexible to meet the needs and abilities of the students, a well-planned lesson is essential. Without careful planning, little or inadequate learning is likely to occur. For example, if you were a preservice teacher working with the Civil War activity described above and had not carefully planned the group-work, you might stray from the objective—"the students will examine the Civil War from the perspective of various groups of Southerners"—to teach skills that students don't really need to complete the assignment. Although library skills are essential if the students are to find their own references, they are not required if the references are located for the students by the teacher and librarian.

This is part of the reason why reflecting on teaching is critically important. During your reflection, you can remind yourself of what the objective of the lesson had been and assess if it were achieved. If not, you might discover that in the name of flexibility you deserted the objective and inserted a new one—teaching library skills—that might have been more appropriately addressed at another time.

SAMPLE FORM 48

Reflections on Small-Group Teaching

NAME OF PRESERVICE TEACHER: Nezerdine Williams

DATE AND TIME OF RECORD: May 10, 20—, 1:10 p.m.

TEACHER/SCHOOL/GRADE: Mr. Duque, Cliburn Elementary School, Third grade

OBJECTIVE OF LESSON: To think carefully and reflect about your teaching of a small group. Below are some guiding questions/statements you can use for your reflection.

Instructions: Use Form 48A to respond to the following questions after you have completed your small-group teaching.

1. **Select**
   a. What were the characteristics (age, gender, background) of the pupils in your small group?
   b. What concepts/skills did you address?
   c. What performance-based standards (the ten principles) did you address?

2. **Describe**
   a. What diverse student needs did you consider in your planning to teach the small groups?
   b. Briefly describe the resources/materials you used.
   c. How did you address multiple intelligences?
   d. What teaching strategies did you incorporate in your lesson?

3. **Analyze**
   a. How did your assessment of prior student learning influence your lesson?
   b. How did the characteristics of the pupils affect your planning and teaching?
   c. What performance modes did you use (e.g., writing, speaking, art)?
   d. How did you modify your plan and teaching to adjust to the unexpected?

4. **Appraise**
   a. How successful was your teaching? What was most effective? What was least effective?
   b. What did the students learn?

5. **Transform**
   a. What did you learn about selecting and using varied teaching strategies?
   b. What did you learn about planning for teaching a small group?

Source: Adapted from North Carolina State Department of Public Instruction *Performance Based Licensure*, Raleigh, NC, 1998–1999.

Large Groups

After student participants have successfully instructed individuals and small groups of students, they are ready to work with a large group or the entire class. Due to the variety of individuals in a large group of twenty or more students, instruction is not as precise as with individuals and small groups. Learning theorist Robert Gagne in *Principles of Instructional Design* (1979) refers to the teacher's amount of control over instructional events as the "degree of precision" (258). According to Gagne, precision decreases as numbers of students in the instructional group grow. This lack of precision occurs because each student in the large group learns differently, possesses varied prerequisite knowledge, has had different experiences, works at different skill levels, has had varied instructional experiences and successes, possesses differing attitudes about education, has different interests and needs, etc. To increase the teacher's control over classroom events, careful planning that addresses student differences is required.

Getting Started

The more prepared you are to teach a large-group lesson, the less nervous you are likely to be. Confidence comes from knowledge of the subject content and access to and understanding of quality materials. In addition, the prepared preservice teacher knows the students as a result of observation, tutoring, and small-group work that has previously occurred. Further, he or she has planned well and has reflected on those plans and on prior teaching experiences, transforming instruction based on those reflections. Finally, the confident student participant has shared and discussed those plans with the classroom teacher and university instructor. Many successful preservice teachers have practiced and previewed their teaching on video- or audiotape and discussed these presentations with instructors or other trusted mentors or friends.

An excellent way to get started is planning to teach a lesson (or parts of a lesson) on a concept or skill that is particularly familiar to you. For example, if you have spent a semester in Great Britain, a lesson introducing students to the country through slides, music, oral reading, and discussion can be a good initial lesson. The students have an opportunity to learn something about you, and your first teaching experience is likely to be more rewarding since you are already comfortable with the material.

Planning for the Large Group

M. Lee Manning in *Developmentally Appropriate Middle-Level Schools* (1993) suggests that large-group instruction requires careful and effective planning of teaching strategies to match the diverse learning styles within the large group. In other words, teachers must consider the needs of the individual while attempting to help large groups achieve lesson objectives. According to Manning, successful individualization within the large group includes the following:

- questions that progress from requiring factual information to higher levels of synthesis and value judgment (see pp. 29, 30, 31 for information on questioning)
- varieties of advanced organizers (also called "anticipatory set" or "focus") that prepare and motivate students for the new concept or skill
- multisensory experiences that allow students to utilize multiple intelligences such as reading aloud, reading silently, music, artwork, journals, notetaking, computer graphics, etc.
- multiple-review and reflection strategies such as debates, simulations, time-lines, computer software, or journal entries

Many components of the large-group lesson plan are similar to tutoring and small-group plans. However, the large-group plan must recognize the wide variety of learners in the classroom. Here are some steps in the large-group plan.

1. Gaining the attention of the learner is even more important in large-group instruction than in tutoring or small-group instruction, since lack of attention by one or more students in the large group can lead to serious discipline problems. There are many ways to gain the attention of students. Demonstrations, oral readings, audiovisual presentations, provocative questions, and dramatic monologues are a few commonly used techniques.

2. Informing students of the lesson's objective(s) gives the learners a sense of direction and a common goal.

3. Stimulating recall of prerequisite learning is of critical importance, but it is very difficult to do successfully in a large group. Although no approach to helping students recall previous learning can be successful with all students, you can help by:

- reviewing material covered in the previous class
- asking students probing questions
- having students complete short activities or exercises
- requiring students to review their notes early in the class period and frame questions or write a summarizing paragraph based on their notes
- reviewing homework assignments from previous classes, etc.

4. Presenting the new material to be learned should emphasize distinctive features of the new concept or skill (Gagne 1979, 254). For example, if the students have been working in the library to develop research skills and have just completed using the card catalog to locate books on a particular topic, the new lesson might involve using the *Guide to Periodical Literature* to discover information about their topic.

5. Particularly, care in presenting new material in classes in which special students are included is critical. Student participants must be aware of whether these learners lack the background information or have the skills they need to complete a task or assignment. Within the lesson, the student participant must provide for the needs of these learners by including definitions or descriptions, providing examples or sets of procedures, providing visuals to reinforce the concept, providing computer reinforcement, or repeating key information so that it can be communicated to the learner.

6. Using a variety of techniques to provide learning guidance for all kinds of learners and multiple intelligences is a necessary part of lesson planning. For example, if the new concept deals with a historic event, there are numerous ways to help learners understand the event. These include:

- showing pictures (still or motion) of it
- placing it on a class-constructed timeline
- having the students research various aspects of the event
- conducting a simulation of the event
- having small groups prepare dramatic episodes
- orally reading eyewitness accounts of the event, etc.

If learners use all of their senses in dealing with a new skill or concept, they are more likely to retain it. The use of all the senses requires active participation by each learner during a significant part of every lesson. During periods of time in which learners are working in small groups or independently, the student participant must be aware of the needs of special students. It may be necessary to provide:

- peer tutors
- special books
- computer-assisted instructional programs
- cassette recordings of instructions, etc.

These instructional modifications should be described in each special student's Individualized Educational Plan (see Sample IEP Form 33, Chapter Four, pp. 81, 82).

7. Providing feedback in each lesson lets learners know if they are reaching the objective. This can be accomplished by using a variety of techniques such as quizzes, student board-work, exercises, activities, tests, assignments, question-and-answer sessions, small-group

or individual oral reports, student-teacher conferences (these can be as short as a few seconds as the teacher circulates throughout the room commenting on each student's work), etc.

8. Assisting the learner in retention and transfer of concepts and skills is an important part of effective teaching. This can be done through techniques such as reviews; written student summarization of major concepts (precise writing); student notetaking and instruction in how to take effective notes; construction of appropriate timelines, charts, or graphs, etc.

Following is a checklist of additional helpful hints for teaching large groups.

SAMPLE FORM 49

Checklist for Working with Large Groups

STUDENT: Amy Poulimenos

TEACHER: Mrs. Garner

GRADE LEVEL AND/OR SUBJECT: Eleventh grade; biology

DATES: October 17, 20—October 19, 20—

OBJECTIVE: To practice my teaching/management skills with a large group

Instructions to Student Participant: As you complete each of these activities, place a check [✓] in the right-hand column.

Activity	Completed
Management of the Classroom	
1. Discuss management rules with the classroom teacher.	✓
2. Ascertain consequences for infractions with the classroom teacher.	✓
3. Use only the discipline methods sanctioned by the classroom teacher and the school.	✓
4. Communicate the rules and consequences to the students so that they know you will enforce them.	✓
5. Enforce rules and apply consequences consistently.	didn't work one time
6. Do not threaten if you do not intend to carry through on the threat (e.g., "If you aren't quiet, I'll keep you all after school.").	✓
7. Make eye contact with as many students as possible.	✓
8. Call students by name. (Make a temporary seating chart to help you learn names or have the students make, wear, or display name tags.)	✓ ✓
Teaching	
1. Carefully plan lessons and divide them into clear segments. (Use a planning format such as those in Chapter Five, pp. 33, 34, 35)	✓
2. Be sure all materials are copied and ready to distribute.	✓
3. Preview all materials prior to using or showing them.	✓
4. Preread anything you intend to use.	✓
5. Maintain instructional momentum. (i.e., Keep up the pace; do not spend too long on any one element of the plan; do not overexplain.)	✓

Activity	Completed
6. Be certain that students understand what is expected (i.e., Ask them to explain to you what they are to do; place assignments on the chalkboard prior to the lesson; make sure instructions and printing on handouts are clear; provide clear examples).	✓
7. Be sure students know how to perform and are capable of accomplishing the task. (Beware of asking students to do tasks for which they do not have prerequisite knowledge or skills; check with the classroom teacher to be sure they will be able to accomplish what you expect.)	✓
8. Review previous lessons and prerequisite knowledge or skills required for this lesson.	✓
9. Actively involve the students in the lesson.	✓
10. Use teaching methodology appropriate to the subject and the maturity of the students (e.g., labs in science classes, oral reading and independent writing in English and language arts, problem solving in mathematics, research in social studies, etc.).	Tried, the teacher said I did
11. Employ a variety of teaching techniques so that all types of learners can achieve (e.g., audiovisuals, hands-on activities, problem solving, student-designed charts and graphs, laboratories, demonstrations, etc.).	✓
12. Assess students' level of mastery of skills and concepts as often as possible (e.g., classwork that requires demonstration of mastery, observation of students completing classwork, homework that is not merely drill, quizzes, journal entries, writing assignments, etc.).	✓
13. Expect mastery of skills and concepts after a period of teaching, practice, coaching, assessing, reteaching, etc.	n/a
14. Do not expect all students to master all concepts and skills in the same way or at the same time. Group students to provide additional assistance to those who have not mastered important concepts and skills. Use different teaching techniques with these students, or allow those who have mastered the skills or concepts to tutor those who have not.	✓

After teaching the lesson you will want to reflect on what was successful and what was less than successful. To help you do this, we have provided a reflection form below.

SAMPLE FORM 50

Reflections on Large-Group Teaching

TEACHER: Inez Jenkins

DATE AND TIME OF RECORD: May 22, 20—, 10:50 a.m.

GRADE LEVEL AND/OR SUBJECT: Eleventh grade; chemistry

OBJECTIVE: To think carefully and reflect on your teaching a large group. Below are some guiding questions/statements you can use for your reflection.

Instructions: You will use Form 50A, p. 208 to respond to the questions.

continued

1. **Select**
   a. What concepts/skills did you address in the lesson?
   b. Why did you address these concepts/skills?
   c. How do these concepts/skills relate to the students' age group?

2. **Describe**
   a. Briefly describe the characteristics of the students (gender, age, race, ability levels).
   b. What resources/materials did you use?
   c. What multiple intelligences did you address?
   d. What role(s) (coach, audience, facilitator) did you play to encourage student learning?
   e. What teaching strategies did you incorporate?
   f. What student assessment technique(s) did you use prior to planning your lesson?
   g. What assessment of students' learning did you apply at the conclusion of your lesson?

3. **Analyze**
   a. How did the characteristics of the students affect your lesson plan?
   b. How did you utilize different performance modes (writing, speaking, reading, doing experiments, solving puzzles)? Why?
   c. Did you modify your plan because of unanticipated events? How?
   d. Why did you select the particular teaching and assessment strategies you incorporated in your lesson?
   e. Evaluate the assessment strategies you used in your lesson.

4. **Appraise**
   a. How successful was your lesson? What was most effective? Least effective?
   b. How did your choice of teaching strategies increase the students' opportunities to engage in critical thinking and problem solving?

5. **Transform**
   a. What did you learn from planning your lesson? What did you learn from teaching the lesson?
   b. What did you learn about the teaching strategies you used?
   c. How did you adjust instruction as a result of the assessment of student learning?

Source: Adapted from North Carolina State Department of Public Instruction. *Performance Based Licensure*, Raleigh, NC, 1998–1999.

PART IV

The Portfolio

Chapter Seven
Keeping a Portfolio

Definition of a Portfolio

Portfolio development is common to many professionals. Artists, designers, architects, authors, entertainers, scientists, and university faculty are some of the professionals who keep records of their work and achievements in a portfolio. The portfolio may contain items such as pictures of or actual samples of the individual's work. In addition, audio- or videotapes documenting the work may be included. Letters commending the individual's achievements, copies of articles either written by or about the individual, and testimonials from those familiar with the work may also be prominent in the portfolio. Results of laboratory experiments may be included as might solutions to difficult mathematical problems. Finally other displays, problems, solutions, etc., designed to show the quality of the work can be included. In short, you might think of a portfolio as a professional scrapbook, or as educator and researcher Sandra M. Murphy says, a "collection" that illustrates your history and your success. (1998, 7)

It is important to note that a portfolio is a professional document designed to highlight an individual's professional development and achievement. Therefore, many items that would be found in a personal scrapbook are inappropriate in a portfolio. In addition to illustrating an individual's career, a portfolio exhibits the person's ability to reflect, appropriately assess professional strengths, and organize.

Until recently, teachers who kept portfolios kept them for personal reasons much as one would have a scrapbook or a diary. However, with the advent of teacher accountability, assessment, and national licensure of teachers, professional portfolios are increasingly important in the teaching profession. Because development of a portfolio is time consuming, difficult, and important to your career advancement, we have included this new chapter in the text.

Educator and researcher Lee Shulman of Stanford University introduced the idea of portfolio development in teacher education and assessment in the early 1990s. According to Shulman, "A teaching portfolio is the structured, documentary history of a set of coached or mentored acts of teaching substantiated by student work and fully realized through reflective writing, deliberation, and serious conversation" (1994, 37). Educators Diane Hood Nettles and Pamela Bondi Petrick have developed a similar definition for use by preservice teachers. "Preservice education portfolios are collections of authentic, learner-specific documents that give evidence of growth and development toward becoming teachers. The portfolios are also an acknowledgment that teacher development is an individualized process. They reflect a student's progress over time, and help document if goals are being met in teacher preparation" (1995, 10).

Purpose of a Portfolio

First and foremost, a portfolio is used to document professional growth. Keeping a portfolio should be viewed as a rewarding activity. Like most rewarding tasks it is complex, perplexing, and time-consuming. A portfolio should not be looked at as something that can be quickly thrown together.

A teaching portfolio is an organizational and assessment tool. It allows you to integrate the INTASC performance-based standards; your work in observation, participation, and teaching; and reflections about your work. Many of the forms you have completed as you have worked through this text can be placed in your portfolio to illustrate your progress in becoming a teacher. Your portfolio should not be designed to illustrate a finished product but rather to reflect a work in progress. That work is your professional development as a teacher. Keep in mind that the standards under which you will be evaluated for much of your career assume that teaching is developmental in nature. Part of that development involves keeping a portfolio that allows you to document, and others to examine, your growth as a professional.

A teaching portfolio is a reflective tool. As you collect and organize artifacts (samples and examples of your work and your students' work) and documents (lesson plans, management strategies, teacher-designed tests, etc.), you will begin to see patterns related to your teaching. You may discover, for example, that you have successfully documented student diversity. However, you may have failed to successfully take into account diversity in your teaching. Reflection on and discussion of this problem with your mentors may lead you to conclude that you need to transform your planning to include, for example, unit plans that incorporate multiple strategies, modes of learning, and varieties of materials over a period of time.

A teaching portfolio requires analysis. You must analyze which of the many artifacts and documents related to your teaching and your students' learning should be included in your portfolio. Through this process, you are developing a rationale of what is important to you as a teacher.

A teaching portfolio leads to the development of a rationale and philosophy. Philosophers have told us for centuries that it is the purposeful, reflective life that is worth living. We know that we are happiest and most fulfilled when we are striving toward clearly understood goals. When we reach those goals, we must have new ones in order to remain truly happy. In addition, goals by themselves are not motivators—there must be a reason to achieve the goal. The same is true in our professional lives—whether teaching or any other career. It is critical that we know why we are teaching and what we plan to achieve. Portfolios will help you focus on what is truly important. By focusing on important issues, ideas, artifacts, and documents you will begin to develop a real rationale for teaching and a philosophy of learning.

A teaching portfolio leads to an understanding of the importance of reflective practice. If you have been a good student, you have reflected on how a final exam or project has assisted you in tying together what may have previously appeared to be disparate concepts and skills within a subject. The same type of synthesis occurs in the process of developing a portfolio. You will begin to understand the importance of the observation that you have completed and reflected upon. Likewise, you will understand why you first worked with individual pupils, then small groups, and finally the entire class. You will know why you conducted assessments of your students. In short, you will begin to understand the importance of your entire teacher-education program.

Steps in Preparing a Portfolio

It is critical that you remember that portfolio preparation is an ongoing project. Even though this is the final chapter of the text, you have been preparing your portfolio from the day you completed your first observations. The process now is an organizational one. Below are some suggestions to help you get started.

1. Use the ten performance-based principles to organize your portfolio (pp. 37, 38, 39). Use one notebook or folder for each principle. The principles will not only serve as an organizational tool, but also as criteria for the selection of artifacts and documents to keep in your portfolio.

2. Sort through all of the forms from this text that you have completed during your observation, preteaching, planning, and teaching experiences. If you have been assigned other forms to complete, sort through those as well. Place each form in its most appropriate file or notebook. This process involves reflection and consultation with peers, classroom teachers, university professors and/or supervisors, and other trusted mentors.

3. Select documents or artifacts to illustrate important aspects of your development as a teacher. Documents might include unit and lesson plans. Artifacts might include photographs taken of the classroom and students, samples of student work, examples of tests you designed, results of student assessments, etc. If you have audio- or videotaped your teaching, you may also want to include those tapes in your portfolio. **WARNING:** Do not attempt to include everything you and your students have done. An important part of this process is reflecting on what is most important and illustrative. Keep in mind that people do not want to examine your entire life's history; rather, they want you to help them understand what is important to you.

4. Write a brief rationale for each notebook or folder explaining why you have selected the particular forms, documents, and artifacts. Also, state why the items you have chosen fit into the particular performance-based standard. (Note: It is possible that some items might be illustrative of more than one standard. This is why your rationale is important.)

5. Write an introduction to your entire portfolio. This introduction might be the beginning step toward developing a philosophy of teaching and learning.

6. Write a reflection on what you have learned about teaching and learning. You might want to include one reflection for each of the ten principles, or your reflection might be the conclusion of the entire portfolio. (Note: It may be helpful to complete this step prior to writing your introduction.)

7. Discuss your portfolio with your cooperating teacher, professor, supervisor, peers, or other mentors. Consider the discussion to be a part of the portfolio development process.

8. Present your portfolio to your teacher-education class or seminar. Learning how to present it requires additional reflection. The presentation will be terribly boring if you simply go through your portfolio saying, "And then . . . and then . . ." Instead, you must select the most important items illustrating your growth as a teacher and present those in an entertaining manner. Oral presentation is a reflection of you as a teacher.

Below is a form that will help you reflect on the practice of developing a portfolio.

SAMPLE FORM 51

Reflections on Keeping a Portfolio

NAME OF PRESERVICE TEACHER: Angela Harris

NAME OF CLASSROOM TEACHER: Mrs. Jones

NAME OF SCHOOL: Meredith Elementary

DATE(S) OF PREPARING THE PORTFOLIO: November 11, 20— December 15, 20—

OBJECTIVE: To think carefully and reflect on the planning and preparation of a portfolio.

continued

Instructions: Make a list of the ten performance-based standards (Chapter Two, pp. 37, 38, 39). Refer to them as you respond to the statements/questions as given below. After you have completed your portfolio, respond to the statements/questions on Form 51A, p. 209.

1. **Select**
   a. What was your objective for preparing a portfolio?
   b. How did you organize your portfolio?

2. **Describe**
   a. List the observation, participation and teaching forms, documents, and artifacts which you selected for inclusion in your portfolio.
   b. Briefly describe assistance you received from classroom teachers, university professors, and peers.
   c. Briefly describe any problems/concerns you experienced.

3. **Analyze**
   a. How did your reflections on completed observations, participation, and teaching help or hinder you as you prepared your portfolio?
   b. How did you decide which forms, documents, or artifacts related to each performance-based standard?

4. **Appraise**
   a. How effective were you in relating your work to the ten performance indicators from the INTASC standards?
   b. How successful were you in keeping a portfolio?

5. **Transform**
   a. What did you learn about teaching from keeping a portfolio?
   b. What did you learn about yourself as a preservice/future classroom teacher?

Source: Adapted from North Carolina State Department of Public Instruction. *Performance Based Licensure*, Raleigh, NC, 1998–1999.

The Portfolio and Your Future Career

There are many reasons why keeping a portfolio during your preservice teaching is important to your future. First, a portfolio, rather than a résumé, is far more illustrative of who you are as a professional. The fact that you have compiled a portfolio puts you ahead of those candidates for teaching positions who have not completed one. It shows school administrators that you are a reflective practitioner. It also tells administrators that you are on your way to achieving national licensure that requires portfolio development. (Remember: If you present the portfolio during the interview process, prepare your presentation so that you highlight the portfolio's key elements. If the interviewer wants more information, he or she can request to review your portfolio. Of course, you must be prepared to leave it with the interviewer for a reasonable amount of time.)

Although a well-done portfolio is an important job-search tool, there are other more important reasons for preparing one. The process of portfolio organization increases your chances of professional growth during your preservice training. The processes of organizing a portfolio and writing rationales require you to reflect on your practice. In addition, the process helps you see clearly what your students have learned and what you have accomplished. In addition, it assists you in tying together numerous bits and pieces of important information, documents, and artifacts that can be lost in the day-to-day pressures of observing, planning, and teaching.

Just as you must decide what techniques to use in encouraging the development of skills in your students, so, too, your university professors and supervisors must do the same. They know what you will come to understand: Portfolio preparation requires the utilization of high-level, cognitive skills. In preparing a successful portfolio, you are analyzing, making decisions, categorizing, organizing, reflecting, creating, and interacting with others about your work. If you present the portfolio, you are honing these skills even more. Likewise, you are improving your oral communication. All of these skills are critical for high levels of achievement as a teacher.

In addition, your portfolio gives you something to take with you when you begin teaching. Many of the successful unit and lesson plans you created may be able to be adapted to your first classroom. Some of the materials you used may also be applicable. The assessment tools may be transferable to new situations. Even if none of what you created is useable in your new environment with a new, diverse student population, your reflections and the habits you have formed will be.

Finally, the portfolio gives you tangible evidence of your work and professional growth during the semesters you spend observing, planning, and finally teaching. It allows you to share your experiences with friends, family, mentors, and professional colleagues.

PART V

Glossary

Glossary

NOTE: *The number(s) that follow(s) each definition refer to the text. For additional information on each entry, see the referenced page(s).*

Anecdotal observation-a written account of an observed classroom event, a student, or the teaching of a lesson for a specified period of time. 18

Degree of precision-Knowing how to manage a variety of instructional events in large-group instruction. 115

Large-group instruction-Using carefully detailed teaching strategies to match the diversity of learners in a large group. 115, 116, 117, 118, 119

Lesson plan-A carefully planned design for a specific educational event, including objectives, motivation, teaching techniques, materials, practice, feedback, and review. 33, 34, 35

Multiple intelligences-The ten types of student intelligences as identified by Howard Gardner, indicating the diverse nature of human intelligence rather than just the singular IQ. 54, 55

Objective observations-Observing the entire event, setting goals, and recording information completely, accurately, and objectively. 18

Participating-Assisting in a variety of noninstructional duties, then moving to instructional duties, such as tutoring. 89, 90, 91

Planning-Following a series of specifically designed steps in a particular lesson plan format. 95, 96, 97, 98

Portfolio-A collection of documents that give evidence of growth and development toward becoming a teacher. 123, 124, 125

Reflections-Looking back on one's observations, participation, and teaching to assess strengths and weaknesses for further growth and development. 9, 10, 11

Small-group instruction-Teaching a small group using a completed lesson plan. 111, 112, 113

Standards-A common core of teaching knowledge as expressed in ten performance-based principles to be acquired by all teachers. 36, 37, 38, 39

Structured observations-Objective observations of a predetermined classroom event, student, or teacher in which data are recorded, using a prepared format such as a checklist. 24, 33

Systematic observations-Planned, objective, goal-oriented observations of different classroom situations over an extended period of time. 18

Teaching styles-The unique way in which an individual teacher organizes instruction, based on his/her philosophy of teaching and learning. 32

Tutoring—Formal-A series of well-planned lessons after first diagnosing the strengths and weaknesses of a student. 105, 106

Tutoring—Informal-Short-term teaching that usually guides one student in learning specific tasks, such as writing a story. 104, 105

PART VI

Forms

FORM 1A

Anecdotal Record Form for Observing Teachers or Instructional Events—1

NAME OF OBSERVER: _____

DATE AND TIME OF OBSERVATION: _____

LENGTH OF OBSERVATION: _____

PERSON AND/OR EVENT OBSERVED: _____

GRADE LEVEL AND/OR SUBJECT: _____

OBJECTIVE OF OBSERVATION: _____

_____

Instructions to the Observer: As completely and accurately as possible, describe the person or the event. If appropriate, include direct quotes and descriptions of the location or individual. Try to avoid making judgments.

FORM 2A

Anecdotal Teacher-Student Interaction Form

NAME OF OBSERVER: _____

DATE AND TIME OF OBSERVATION: _____

LENGTH OF OBSERVATION: _____

TEACHER: _____

STUDENT: _____

GRADE LEVEL AND/OR SUBJECT: _____

OBJECTIVE OF OBSERVATION: _____

Instructions to the Observer: As completely and accurately as possible, describe the interactions between the teacher and one selected student. Include direct quotes and descriptions of the teacher and the student, including facial expressions, gestures, and voice quality. However, be careful to avoid making judgments.

Time	Teacher	Student

FORM 3A

Anecdotal Record Form for Observing Teachers or Instructional Events—2

NAME OF OBSERVER: _____

DATE AND TIME OF OBSERVATION: _____

LENGTH OF OBSERVATION: _____

PERSON AND/OR EVENT OBSERVED: _____

GRADE LEVEL AND/OR SUBJECT: _____

OBJECTIVE OF OBSERVATION: _____

Instructions to the Observer: As completely and accurately as possible, describe the person or the event. If appropriate, include direct quotes and descriptions of the location or the individual. Try to avoid making judgments.

FORM 4A

Anecdotal Record Form for Grouping Patterns

NAME OF OBSERVER: _____

DATE AND TIME OF OBSERVATION: _____

LENGTH OF OBSERVATION: _____

PERSON AND/OR EVENT OBSERVED: _____

GRADE LEVEL AND/OR SUBJECT: _____

OBJECTIVE OF OBSERVATION: _____

_____

Instructions to the Observer: As completely and accurately as possible, describe the different groups in the classroom. If appropriate, include direct quotes and descriptions of locations or individuals. Try to avoid making judgments.

FORM 5A

Observation Form for Rank Ordering

NAME OF OBSERVER: _____

DATE AND TIME OF OBSERVATION: _____

LENGTH OF OBSERVATION: _____

TECHNIQUES OR TYPES OBSERVED: _____

GRADE LEVEL AND/OR SUBJECT: _____

OBJECTIVE OF OBSERVATION: _____

Instructions to the Observer: List a variety of possible techniques or types of grouping patterns. Keep a tally of those you observe. At the end of the observation period, count the number of occurrences of each technique or type.

Techniques or Types of Grouping Patterns	Number of Occurrences
Total Number of Groups (Date:)	

FORM 6A

Coding System—Type and Tally
of Student-Teacher Interaction

NAME OF OBSERVER: _____

DATE AND TIME OF OBSERVATION: _____

LENGTH OF OBSERVATION: _____

ELEMENT OBSERVED: _____

TEACHER AND/OR STUDENT: _____

GRADE LEVEL AND/OR SUBJECT: _____

OBJECTIVE OF OBSERVATION: _____

_____

Instructions to the Observer: Tally the number of times each interactive behavior occurs during your observation period. Try to record at least one example of each type of interaction. At the end of the observation period, total the number of all teacher-student interactions, and calculate the percentage of the total for each interaction.

Type of Interactive Behavior	Tally of Times Observed	Percentage

INDIRECT
 	
 Accepts Feelings
   Example:
 	
 Praises/Encourages
   Example:
 	
 Accepts or Uses Student Ideas
   Example:
 	
 Asks Questions
   Example:		

Type of Interactive Behavior	Tally of Times Observed	Percentage
DIRECT *Lectures* Example:		
Gives Directions Example:		
Criticizes or Justifies Authority Example:		
STUDENT TALK *Student Talk-Response* Example:		
Student Talk-Initiation Example:		
TOTALS		
MOST FREQUENTLY USED TYPE OF INTERACTION		

Source: Adapted from Ned Flanders, 1985.

FORM 7A

Observation Form for Examining Questions

NAME OF OBSERVER: _____

DATE AND TIME OF OBSERVATION: _____

TEACHER: _____

GRADE LEVEL AND/OR SUBJECT: _____

OBJECTIVE OF OBSERVATION: _____

_____

Instructions to the Observer: On a separate piece of paper or on a cassette, record all questions asked by the teacher, orally and in writing, for one lesson. Then place each question below at the appropriate level. Next, tally the number of questions at each level. Count the total number of questions asked, and compute a percentage for each level.

Type of Question	Total Number of Questions
1. Memory:	
2. Translation:	
3. Interpretation:	

Type of Question	Total Number of Questions
4. Application:	
5. Analysis:	
6. Synthesis:	
7. Evaluation:	
TOTAL Number of Questions, All Levels:	

Percentage of Memory _____ ; Translation _____ ; Interpretation _____ ; Application _____ ;
Analysis _____ ; Synthesis _____ ; Evaluation _____

FORM 8A

Checklist for Determining Teaching Style

NAME OF OBSERVER: _____

DATE AND TIME OF OBSERVATION: _____

TEACHER: _____

GRADE LEVEL AND/OR SUBJECT: _____

OBJECTIVE OF OBSERVATION: _____

_____

Instructions to the Observer: Prior to the observation, read over the items below. These items represent various teaching styles used by teachers. During and after the observation, place an "x" next to those items you have observed.

___ prefers teaching situations that allow interaction and discussion with students	___ prefers impersonal teaching situations
___ uses questions to check on student learning following instruction	___ uses questions to introduce topics and probe student answers
___ viewed by students as teaching facts	___ uses teacher-organized learning situations
___ provides less feedback, avoids negative evaluation	___ viewed by students as encouraging to apply principles
___ strong in establishing a warm and personal learning environment	___ gives corrective feedback, uses negative evaluation
	___ strong in organizing and guiding student learning

Source: [on-line] Internet path: http:// www.ais.missstate.edu.\ALS/Unit9modulers.num and Dean Boyd, computer systems coordinator, Mississippi State University of Starkville, MS, College of Agriculture and Life Sciences, September 22, 1999.

FORM 9A

Observation Form for Structured Observation of a Lesson

NAME OF OBSERVER: _____

DATE AND TIME OF OBSERVATION: _____

TEACHER: _____

GRADE LEVEL AND/OR SUBJECT: _____

OBJECTIVE OF OBSERVATION: _____

Instructions to the Observer: As you observe in the classroom, list the elements of the lesson under the categories below. A description of each category appears in italics. List the elements of the lesson on a separate page.

1. **Anticipatory Set**—*In every lesson, the teacher provides initial motivation and focus for the lesson. Sometimes this focus takes the form of a review of previous knowledge important to this lesson; at other times it is designed to "grab" the students' attention. Key words: alerting, relevance, relationship (to previous lesson), meaningfulness, etc.*

2. **Objective**—*In almost every lesson, the teacher specifies the behaviors the students will be expected to perform. In other words, the students know what is expected of them and what they are expected to learn.*

3. **Teacher Input**—*In most lessons, the teacher will provide the students with the information needed to reach the objective successfully. Sometimes, the teacher will show the students how to accomplish the task by modeling appropriate performance.*

4. **Checking for Understanding**—*Throughout the lesson, the teacher checks to ensure that the students understand the concepts or skills being taught. This can be accomplished through random questioning or individual tutoring.*

5. **Guided Practice**—*In every lesson, students practice the expected performance. This may include exercises completed with the teacher, examples done by students on the board, students reading aloud, students working together to complete assignments, games that allow the students to exhibit understanding, etc.*

6. **Independent Practice**—*Student independently exhibit the behaviors set forth in the objective. To accomplish this, students might complete problems, write a paper, do an experiment, give a report, complete a project, do research, etc.*

7. **Closure**—*The teacher helps students review what they have learned in the lesson. This may include a summary of the lesson, questions about what happened during the students' independent practice, the students' report of their progress, an evaluation by the teacher, a discussion of the relationship of this lesson to the next lesson or the unit, or an assignment of additional independent practice.*

Source: Lois Sprinthall. A Strategy Guide for Teachers: Guide Book for Supervisors of Novice Teachers. Unpublished manuscript. Based on the work of Madeline Hunter.

FORM 10A

Checklist of Interview Techniques

NAME OF OBSERVER: _____

DATE, TIME, AND PLACE OF OBSERVATION: _____

PERSON TO BE INTERVIEWED: _____

GRADE LEVEL AND/OR SUBJECT: _____

OBJECTIVE OF OBSERVATION: _____

_____

Instructions to the Observer: Review this checklist prior to and after your interview. Check off those items you have completed.

1. **Prior to the Interview**

____ Establish the purpose for the interview.

____ Request an appointment (time and place), giving sufficient lead time for you and the person to be interviewed.

____ Plan objective, specific questions related to the purpose of the interview.

____ Prioritize questions, asking the most important first.

____ Remind the person to be interviewed of the time, place, and purpose of the interview.

2. **The Interview**

____ Arrive at the pre-established place several minutes before the scheduled time for the interview.

____ Start the interview by reminding the person to be interviewed of its purpose.

____ Request permission to tape the interview (if appropriate).

____ If taping is unfeasible, take careful, objective notes, trying to list direct quotes as often as possible.

____ Avoid inserting impressions or judgments.

____ Limit the interview to no more than 15–30 minutes.

3. **After the Interview**

____ Review with the respondent what has been said or heard.

____ Express your appreciation for the interview.

____ Offer to share the interview report with the respondent.

FORM 11A

A Rating Scale for Observation of Standards for Teaching

NAME OF OBSERVER: _____

DATE AND TIME OF OBSERVATION: _____

LENGTH OF OBSERVATION: _____

TEACHER: _____

GRADE LEVEL OF OBSERVATION: _____

OBJECTIVE OF OBSERVATION: _____

_____

Instruction to the Observer: Prior to your observation, read over each principle carefully. During and after your observation, put a check on the rating scale that best describes what you observed. The check may be either on or between the numbers 1–5. Note: This rating is based on one limited observation.

Content Pedagogy

Principle 1: The teacher understands the central concepts, tools of inquiry, and structures of the discipline(s) he or she teaches and can create learning experiences that make these aspects of subject matter meaningful to students.

1	2	3	4	5
Limited sophistication		Moderate sophistication		High sophistication

Student Development

Principle 2: The teacher understands how children learn and develop and can provide learning opportunities that support their intellectual, social, and personal development.

1	2	3	4	5
Limited sophistication		Moderate sophistication		High sophistication

Diverse Learners

Principle 3: The teacher understands how students differ in their approaches to learning and creates instructional opportunities that are adapted to diverse learners.

1	2	3	4	5
Limited sophistication		Moderate sophistication		High sophistication

continued

Multiple Instructional Strategies

Principle 4: The teacher understands and uses a variety of instructional strategies to encourage students' development of critical thinking, problem solving, and performance skills.

1	2	3	4	5
Limited sophistication		Moderate sophistication		High sophistication

Motivation and Management

Principle 5: The teacher uses an understanding of individual and group motivation and behavior to create a learning environment that encourages positive social interaction, active engagement in learning, and self-motivation.

1	2	3	4	5
Limited sophistication		Moderate sophistication		High sophistication

Communication and Technology

Principle 6: The teacher uses knowledge of effective verbal, nonverbal, and media communication techniques to foster active inquiry, collaboration, and supportive interaction in the classroom.

1	2	3	4	5
Limited sophistication		Moderate sophistication		High sophistication

Planning

Principle 7: The teacher plans instruction based on knowledge of subject matter, students, the community, and curriculum goals.

1	2	3	4	5
Limited sophistication		Moderate sophistication		High sophistication

Assessment

Principle 8: The teacher understands and uses formal and informal assessment strategies to evaluate and ensure the continuous intellectual, social, and physical development of the learner.

1	2	3	4	5
Limited sophistication		Moderate sophistication		High sophistication

Reflective Practice
Principle 9: The teacher is a reflective practitioner who continually evaluates the effects of his or her choices and actions on others (students, parents, and other professionals in the learning community) and who actively seeks out opportunities to grow professionally.

1	2	3	4	5
Limited sophistication		Moderate sophistication		High sophistication

School and Community Development
Principle 10: The teacher fosters relationships with school colleagues, parents, and agencies in the larger community to support students' learning and well-being.

1	2	3	4	5
Limited sophistication		Moderate sophistication		High sophistication

Source: Robert F. Yinger. "The Role of Standards in Teaching and Teacher Education" in *The Education of Teachers*. National Society for the Study of Education (NSSE), pp. 100–101, 1999.

FORM 12 A

Reflective Observation of Teachers

NAME OF OBSERVER: _____

DATE AND TIME OF REFLECTIVE OBSERVATION: _____

TEACHER: _____

GRADE LEVEL AND/OR SUBJECT: _____

OBJECTIVE OF OBSERVATION: _____

_____

Instructions to the Observer: On a separate sheet of paper respond to the following questions:

1. **Select**
   a. What two types of observation did you complete?
   b. What principles from INTASC standards did you address?

2. **Describe**
   a. What grade level(s) did you observe?
   b. Briefly describe your anecdotal observations.
   c. Briefly describe your structured observations.
   d. Briefly describe the type of assessments you used.

3. **Analyze**
   a. How did your prior experience with observation of teachers influence this experience?
   b. How will your observation of different teaching styles affect your future teaching?

4. **Appraise**
   a. Describe the teacher-student interaction you observed. Was it appropriate?
   b. Did the ten principles based on the common core of standards (INTASC) influence your decision to become a teacher? Explain.

5. **Transform**
   a. What did you learn about teaching through your observation?
   b. What did you learn about types of assessment?
   c. How do you think this observation will help you in your future teaching?

Source: Adapted from North Carolina State Department of Public Instruction. *Performance Based Licensure.* Raleigh, NC, 1998–1999:

FORM 13A

Form for Anecdotal Record of Classroom Organization

NAME OF OBSERVER: _____

DATE AND TIME OF OBSERVATION: _____

LENGTH OF OBSERVATION: _____

PERSON AND/OR EVENT OBSERVED: _____

GRADE LEVEL AND/OR SUBJECT: _____

OBJECTIVE OF OBSERVATION: _____

_____

Instructions to the Observer: As completely and accurately as possible, describe the organization of the classroom. Be sure to include as much detail as possible. Try to avoid making judgments.

FORM 14A

Form for a Classroom Map

NAME OF OBSERVER: _____

DATE AND TIME OF OBSERVATION: _____

PERSON AND/OR EVENT OBSERVED: _____

GRADE LEVEL AND/OR SUBJECT: _____

OBJECTIVE OF OBSERVATION: _____

Instructions to the Observer: First, draw a map of the classroom you are observing, including seating arrangements, placement of furniture, computers, telephone, and other equipment. Then, give a brief anecdotal description of these classroom elements: use of technology, lighting, traffic patterns, instructional displays, management, and motivational elements.

1. Draw a classroom map:

2.   Anecdotal description of classroom elements:
     a.   Use of Technology

     b.   Lighting and Traffic Patterns:

     c.   Instructional Displays, Management, and Motivational Elements:

FORM 15A

Form for Coding Scale of Classroom Social Environment

NAME OF OBSERVER: _____

DATE AND TIME OF OBSERVATION: _____

LENGTH OF OBSERVATION: _____

PERSON AND/OR EVENT OBSERVED: _____

GRADE LEVEL AND/OR SUBJECT: _____

OBJECTIVE OF OBSERVATION: _____

Instructions to the Observer: Before using the coding scale, become familiar with each of the fifteen dimensions that describe the classroom social environment on pages 46–47.

Each dimension is divided into three elements (or statements). Each of these three elements appears in the same order, once per set, in the three sets that comprise the coding scale.

To use the coding scale effectively, you should circle the appropriate rating and average the scores *for all three statements* in any given dimension(s) you want to examine. For example, to study classroom diversity, you would compare the scores for numbers 2, 17, and 32.

The scale may also be used to determine what you might want to examine further. Thus, after one or more classroom observations, you may want to average the scores for all three sets, and then pick out those that stand out in some way.

When scoring, you should note the following: (1) some statements are phrased negatively and, thus, their ratings have been reversed, and (2) in several of the dimensions being measured (diversity, speed, difficulty, democracy, and competitiveness), a higher score is not necessarily more desirable.

Dimension Elements	Strongly Disagree	Disagree	Strongly Agree	Agree	No Information
Set 1					
1. A student in this class has the chance to get to know all other students (cohesiveness).	1	2	3	4	N/I
2. The class has students with many different interests (diversity).	1	2	3	4	N/I
3. There is a set of rules for the students to follow (formality).	1	2	3	4	N/I
4. Most of the class has difficulty keeping up with the assigned work (speed).	1	2	3	4	N/I
5. The books and equipment students need or want are easily available in the classroom (environment).	1	2	3	4	N/I
6. There are tensions among certain students that tend to interfere with class activities (friction).	1	2	3	4	N/I
7. Most students have little idea of what the class is attempting to accomplish (goal direction).	4	3	2	1	N/I

Dimension Elements	Strongly Disagree	Disagree	Strongly Agree	Agree	No Information
8. The better students' questions are answered more sympathetically than those of the average students (favoritism).	1	2	3	4	N/I
9. Some students refuse to mix with the rest of the class (cliquishness).	1	2	3	4	N/I
10. The students seem to enjoy their classwork (satisfaction).	1	2	3	4	N/I
11. There are long periods during which the class does nothing (disorganization).	1	2	3	4	N/I
12. Some students in the class consider the work difficult (difficulty).	1	2	3	4	N/I
13. Most students seem to have a concern for the progress of the class (apathy).	4	3	2	1	N/I
14. When group discussions occur, all students tend to contribute (democracy).	1	2	3	4	N/I
15. Most students cooperate rather than compete with one another in this class (competitiveness).	4	3	2	1	N/I

Set 2

Dimension Elements	Strongly Disagree	Disagree	Strongly Agree	Agree	No Information
16. Students in this class are not in close enough contact to develop likes and dislikes for one another (cohesiveness).	4	3	2	1	N/I
17. The class is working toward many different goals (diversity).	1	2	3	4	N/I
18. Students who break the rules are penalized (formality).	1	2	3	4	N/I
19. The class has plenty of time to cover the prescribed amount of work (speed).	4	3	2	1	N/I
20. A comprehensive collection of reference material is available in the classroom for students to use (environment).	1	2	3	4	N/I
21. Certain students seem to have no respect for other students (friction).	1	2	3	4	N/I
22. The objectives of the class are not clearly recognized (goal direction).	4	3	2	1	N/I
23. Every member of the class is given the same privileges (favoritism).	4	3	2	1	N/I
24. Certain students work only with their close friends (cliquishness).	1	2	3	4	N/I
25. There is considerable student dissatisfaction with the classwork (satisfaction).	4	3	2	1	N/I
26. Classwork is frequently interrupted by some students with nothing to do (disorganization).	4	3	2	1	N/I
27. Most students in this class are constantly challenged (difficulty).	1	2	3	4	N/I
28. Some members of the class don't care what the class does (apathy).	1	2	3	4	N/I
29. Certain students have more influence on the class than others (democracy).	4	3	2	1	N/I
30. Most students in the class want their work to be better than their friends' work (competitiveness).	1	2	3	4	N/I

continued

Dimension Elements	Strongly Disagree	Disagree	Strongly Agree	Agree	No Information
Set 3					
31. This class is made up of individuals who do not know each other well (cohesiveness).	4	3	2	1	N/I
32. Different students are interested in different aspects of the class (diversity).	4	3	2	1	N/I
33. There is a right and wrong way of going about class activities (formality).	4	3	2	1	N/I
34. There is little time in this class for daydreaming (speed).	4	3	2	1	N/I
35. There are bulletin board displays and pictures around the room (environment).	4	3	2	1	N/I
36. Certain students in this class are uncooperative (friction).	1	2	3	4	N/I
37. Most of the class realizes exactly how much work is required (goal direction).	1	2	3	4	N/I
38. Certain students in the class are favored over others (favoritism).	1	2	3	4	N/I
39. Most students cooperate equally well with all class members (cliquishness).	4	3	2	1	N/I
40. After an assignment, most students have a sense of satisfaction (satisfaction).	1	2	3	4	N/I
41. The class is well-organized and efficient (disorganization).	4	3	2	1	N/I
42. Most students consider the subject matter easy (difficulty).	4	3	2	1	N/I
43. Students show a common concern for the success of the class (apathy).	4	3	2	1	N/I
44. Each member of the class has as much influence as does any other member (democracy).	4	3	2	1	N/I
45. Students compete to see who can do the best work (competitiveness).	4	3	2	1	N/I

Source: Gary Borich. *Observation Skills for Effective Teaching,* pp. 113–115, 1990.

FORM 16A

Checklist to Determine Student Assessments in the Classroom

NAME OF OBSERVER: _____

DATE/TIME OF OBSERVATION: _____

PERSON AND/OR EVENT OBSERVED: _____

GRADE LEVEL AND/OR SUBJECT: _____

SCHOOL: _____

OBJECTIVE OF OBSERVATION: _____

Instructions to the Observer: After structured observation or an interview with the classroom teacher, put a check in the appropriate column. List additional assessments where required next to items marked with an asterisk.

Type of Assessment	Observed	From Interview

1. Commercial Workbooks in Curricular Areas
    Reading
    Mathematics
    Science
    Social Studies
    Language Arts
    Others* (*handwriting*)		

2. Duplicated Sheets		
3. Homework Assignments		
4. Oral Presentation/Report		

5. Hands-On Performance
    Computers
    Science Experiment
    Construction Project
    Dramatic Performances/Skits
    Chalkboard Work
    Art Project
    Musical Production
    Classroom Displays/Bulletin Board
    School Displays
    Others*		

continued

Type of Assessment	Observed	From Interview

6. Written Work
    Reports
    Research Projects
    Creative Writing
    Others*		

7. Teacher-Made Tests		
8. Prepared Tests From Students' Texts		
9. Standardized Tests		
10. State Competency Tests		
11. State End-of-Year Tests		

12. Anecdotal Records
    Writing Journals/Folders
    Art Folders
    Cumulative Record Folders
    Portfolios
    Others*		

13. Others*		

FORM 17A

Checklist of Goals, Objectives, and Competencies Covered in an Eleventh-Grade History Classroom

NAME OF OBSERVER: _____

DATE AND TIME OF OBSERVATION: _____

TEACHER: _____

SCHOOL: _____

OBJECTIVE OF OBSERVATION: _____

_____

Instructions to the Observer: Use the list of goals and performance indicators from a curriculum guide to develop your own checklist. For an example of a checklist of goals and performance indicators in an eleventh-grade history classroom, see pp. 52, 53. If the competency, goal, objective and/or performance indicator is observed, place an "X" in the right-hand column.

Goals	Performance Indicators	Observed

continued

Goals	Performance Indicators	Observed

FORM 18A

Examination of Curricular Strategies That Challenge Students' Multiple Intelligences

NAME OF OBSERVER: _____

DATE AND TIME OF OBSERVATION: _____

TEACHER: _____

SCHOOL: _____

OBJECTIVE OF OBSERVATION: _____

Instructions to the Observer: A list of curricular descriptors that challenge students' multiple intelligences is given below. Place a check before each descriptor observed.

Visual/Spatial

___ charts
___ graphs
___ photography
___ visual awareness
___ organizers
___ visual metaphors
___ visual analogies
___ visual puzzles
___ 3-D experiences
___ painting
___ illustrations
___ story maps
___ visualizing
___ sketching
___ patterning
___ mind maps
___ color
___ symbols

Logical/Mathematical

___ problem solving
___ tangrams
___ coding
___ geometry
___ measuring
___ classifying
___ predicting
___ logic games
___ data collecting
___ serialing
___ attributes
___ experimenting
___ puzzles
___ manipulatives
___ scientific model
___ money
___ time
___ sequencing
___ critical thinking

Verbal/Linguistic

___ stories
___ retelling
___ journals
___ process writing
___ reader's theatre
___ storytelling
___ choral speaking
___ rehearsed reading
___ bookmaking
___ speaking
___ nonfiction reading
___ research
___ speeches
___ presentations
___ listening
___ reading
___ read-aloud
___ drama

Bodily/Kinesthetic

___ field trips
___ activities
___ creative movement
___ hands-on experiments
___ body language
___ manipulatives
___ physical education
___ crafts
___ drama

Musical/Rhythmic

___ singing
___ humming
___ rhythms
___ rap
___ background music
___ music appreciation
___ mood music
___ patterns
___ form
___ playing instruments

Interpersonal

___ cooperative learning
___ sharing
___ group work
___ peer teaching
___ social awareness
___ conflict mediation
___ discussion
___ peer editing
___ cross-age tutoring
___ social gathering
___ study group
___ clubs
___ brainstorming

Intrapersonal

___ individual study
___ personal goal setting
___ individual projects
___ journal keeping
___ personal choice
___ individualized reading
___ self-esteem activities

Source: Adapted from the Simcoe District School Board. Midhurst, Ontario, Canada, 1996. [on.line] Internet path: http://www.scdsb.on.ca/

FORM 19A

Form for Examining a Curriculum Guide

NAME OF EXAMINER: _____

DATE AND TIME OF EXAMINATION: _____

OBJECTIVE OF EXAMINATION: _____

_____

Instructions to the Examiner: Select a curriculum guide for the grade level and/or subject you will be observing. Complete this short answer survey.

1. Title of the guide: _____

2. Check one: The guide is from the school ____ ; the school district ____ ; the state ____ ; other (specify) _____

3. Date of the guide: _____

4. Grade level(s) of the guide: _____

5. Subject area(s) of the guide: _____

_____

Answer the following yes/no or as indicated:

6. The guide includes: objectives ____ , student activities ____ , resources ____ , examples____ , bibliographies ____ , computer software sources ____ , test banks ____ , discussion questions ____ , material for making transparencies ____ , content outlines ____ , other (specify) _____

7. The guide suggests appropriate textbooks (specify): _____

_____

8. The guide suggests appropriate supplemental books. _____

9. The guide suggests appropriate references. _____

10. The guide suggests activities for different levels of students (i.e. gifted, advanced, basic, etc.) _____

FORM 20A

Checklist for a Multicultural/Antibias Education Evaluation

NAME OF OBSERVER: _____

DATE AND TIME OF OBSERVATION: _____

SCHOOL: _____

GRADE LEVELS OF SCHOOL: _____

OBJECTIVE OF OBSERVATION: _____

_____

Instructions to the Observer: After examining the school's curriculum (using Forms 17 and 19) and observing in numerous classrooms, complete the following evaluation checklist. Place a checkmark below the word or phrase that best describes your observations. Respond only to those items that were observable by you.

1. The classroom environment is reflective of diversity.	Not at all	Some	Large Amount
2. Curriculum focuses on discrete pieces about cultures of various racial and ethnic groups.	Not at all	Some	Large Amount
3. Multicultural activities are added on to the "regular" curriculum (i.e., celebrating various holidays of other cultures).	Not at all	Some	Large Amount
4. Families or caregivers are asked to provide information about the most visible aspects of their cultural heritage (i.e., food, music, and holidays).	Not at all	Some	Large Amount
5. Languages of children (other than English) are used in songs or other communication.	Not at all	Some	Large Amount
6. The curriculum explores cultural differences among the children's families.	Not at all	Some	Large Amount
7. Staff members actively incorporate their children's daily life experiences into daily curriculum.	Not at all	Some	Large Amount
8. Curriculum and teacher-child interactions meet the cultural as well as individual developmental needs of their children.	Not at all	Some	Large Amount
9. Parents' or family caregivers' knowledge about their native cultural background is utilized.	Not at all	Some	Large Amount
10. Staff members intentionally encourage the children's development of critical thinking and tools for resisting prejudice and biased behaviors directed at themselves or others.	Not at all	Some	Large Amount
11. Staff members reflect the cultural and language diversity of the children and families they serve.	Not at all	Some	Large Amount

Source: Adapted from Louise Derman-Sparks. *Young Children*. 54(5):43, Pacific Oaks College, Pasadena, CA, September 1999.

FORM 21A

Form for Technology Usage in the Classroom or Lab

NAME OF OBSERVER: _____

DATE AND TIME OF OBSERVATION: _____

SCHOOL: _____

TEACHER: _____

GRADE LEVEL AND/OR SUBJECT: _____

OBJECTIVE OF OBSERVATION: _____

_____

Instructions to the Observer: It is important to determine whether technology is used to augment instruction in subject areas for the students or whether it is used to teach students technological skills and/or how to use particular applications. Answer the following questions to help identify how technology is being used in the class you are observing.

1. What is the objective(s) of the lesson being observed?

2. Does the use of technology match or reflect the learning objectives for the lesson?

3. How does the use of technology enhance the opportunity for students to meet the lesson's objectives?

4. Is technology used as a teaching tool by the teacher to present concepts and information in a particular subject area?

5. Is technology used to teach computer skills? If so, what skills?

6. Is the teacher's role during the lesson to guide students as they use technology or is his/her role to present information/skills?

7. Is the use of the technology appropriate for the age and skill of the students?

8. Is equitable time provided for all students to use technology?

9. When technology is used, are students engaged in cooperative learning?

10. Is technology introduced for independent use, small-group use, or whole-class use?

11. Does the lesson using technology provide an opportunity for student evaluation or feedback? If so, describe the opportunity. If not, ask the teacher why not.

Source: Jean Camp, Instructional Technology Coordinator, The University of North Carolina at Greensboro. Unpublished. Courtesy of Mary Olson, The University of North Carolina at Greensboro.

FORM 22A

Software Evaluation Form

NAME OF EXAMINER: _____

DATE AND TIME OF EXAMINATION: _____

SOFTWARE TITLE: _____

PUBLISHER: _____

PUBLICATION DATE: _____

OBJECTIVE OF OBSERVATION: _____

_____

Instructions to the Examiner: Determine the parameters of the software package by checking the appropriate blank. Answer the questions on a separate page when necessary. Then rate the product on a scale of 1 to 4 (1 is the lowest and 4 is the highest).

I. **Basic Background Information**

A. Computer Platform:
   IBM ___   Mac ___

B. System Requirements:
   Stand Alone ___   Hard Drive Memory ___
   Networked ___   RAM Memory ___   Both ___

C. Format (check one):
   Disk-Based ___
   CD-ROM ___
   Laserdisc ___

D. Audience:
   PreK–1st ___   9th–12th ___
   2nd–5th ___   Adult ___
   6th–8th ___   Other ___

E. Software Type:
   CAI/Drill and Practice   ___
   Simulations   ___
   Problem-Solving Applications ___
   Game Applications   ___
   Tool Applications   ___
      Database   ___
      Word Processing   ___
      Spreadsheet   ___
   Tutorials   ___
   Grading/Student Information   ___
   Electronic Portfolio Assessment ___
   Electronic Books   ___
      Skill level accommodations ___
   Multimedia authoring   ___
   Telecommunicating   ___

continued

F. Graphics: B/W ___ Color ___ Animation ___

G. Price:

H. Preview Policy: None ___ 30-day ___ Other ___

II. Educational Objectives

A. State Purpose: _____

B. Subject Area Focus:

Math	___	Reading	___	Art	___
Foreign Language	___	Social Studies	___	Science	___
Music	___	Literature	___	Other	___

III. Questions to Consider When Evaluating Software

A. Does the content of the program reflect a sound learning theory? If so, which one? Is the program's subject matter accurate and logically presented?

B. Does the program promote exploration and critical thinking?

C. Does the software span a range of skill abilities?

D. Do students have control of the program? (i.e., Is it self-paced? Can they navigate through the program easily?)

E. Can the program be adapted to large groups, small groups, and individual instruction?

F. Does the program accommodate different ability levels?

G. Does the program provide supportive and positive feedback to students?

H. Are teaching materials provided to accompany the program? If so, describe them.

I. Is the program sensitive to multiculturalism? In what ways?

J. Are the program directions clear enough to be used independently, or does the program require teacher support?

K. Does the school, classroom, or lab have the technical and educational support necessary to maximize the use of the program?

L. Does the program have multimedia features? If so, do they enhance learning?

IV. Rating (Rate items on a scale of 1 to 4; 4 is the highest.)

A. Usability   ___

B. Content   ___

C. Design   ___

D. Difficulty   ___

Source: Designed by Jean Camp, Instructional Technology Coordinator. The University of North Carolina at Greensboro, Unpublished. Courtesy of Mary Olson, The University of North Carolina at Greensboro.

FORM 23A

Checklist for School Personnel Interviews

NAME OF INTERVIEWER: _____

DATES OF INTERVIEWS: _____

SCHOOL: _____

OBJECTIVE OF OBSERVATION: _____

_____

Instructions to the Interviewer: Schedule a conference with an appropriate person from each administrative division of the school. If a specific service is not identified, discuss with the principal or assistant principal how the school provides such a service or otherwise meets the needs of the students. Use checklists I–VI below to (1) formulate your questions and (2) ensure that you ask appropriate questions. You may add some of your own topics to the list. Check off each item for which you obtain an answer. Take notes in the space provided.

I.   Guidance, Testing, Evaluation, and Reporting

NAME OF PERSON INTERVIEWED: _____

TITLE OF PERSON INTERVIEWED: _____

DATE, TIME, AND PLACE OF INTERVIEW: _____

APPROXIMATE LENGTH OF INTERVIEW: _____

____   1. Purpose of guidance program

____   2. Procedures for obtaining services

____   3. Services of guidance program (individual and group)

____   4. Referral services

____   5. Services for pregnant students and single parents

____   6. Teachers' role in guidance

____   7. Students' role in guidance

____   8. Parents' role in guidance

____   9. Standardized tests and purposes

____ 10. School's grading/reporting policies

____ 11. School's promotion/retention policies

____ 12. Academic advising and placement of students

Notes:

II. Library or Media Center/Instructional Materials and Equipment

NAME OF PERSON INTERVIEWED: _____

TITLE OF PERSON INTERVIEWED: _____

DATE, TIME, AND PLACE OF INTERVIEW: _____

APPROXIMATE LENGTH OF INTERVIEW: _____

____ 1. Available library materials related to subject and/or grade level

____ 2. Library or media center hours for students and teachers

____ 3. Procedures for using library or media center (class/students/teachers)

____ 4. Vertical file and appropriate contents

____ 5. Computer indexing of library materials

____ 6. Equipment and media available for teachers' library/media center use

____ 7. Checkout policies for students, teachers, and classes

____ 8. Equipment and media available for classroom use

____ 9. Procedures for instructing students in library/media center use

____ 10. Assistance available for use of equipment and media

____ 11. Availability and procedures for computer use by students and teachers

____ 12. Procedures for selection and review of library materials and media

Notes:

III. Health Services

NAME OF PERSON INTERVIEWED: _____

TITLE OF PERSON INTERVIEWED: _____

DATE, TIME, AND PLACE OF INTERVIEW: _____

APPROXIMATE LENGTH OF INTERVIEW: _____

___ 1. Available health services at school

___ 2. Services available through school referral

___ 3. Sex education and condom distribution

___ 4. Services for pregnant students

___ 5. Procedures for teacher with ill/injured child

___ 6. Procedures for dealing with HIV-positive student

___ 7. School safety precautions, policies, and regulations

___ 8. Other county/community services available to students

___ 9. Health and related issues taught in classes

Notes:

continued

IV. Curriculum Resource Person or Assistant Principal for Curriculum

NAME OF PERSON INTERVIEWED: _____

TITLE OF PERSON INTERVIEWED: _____

DATE, TIME, AND PLACE OF INTERVIEW: _____

APPROXIMATE LENGTH OF INTERVIEW: _____

____ 1. School, district, county, or state curriculum guides

____ 2. Multicultural aspects of the curriculum

____ 3. School's organization for instruction:

      ____ a. grouping

      ____ b. departmentalization

      ____ c. chain of command

      ____ d. curricular offerings

      ____ e. extracurricular offerings

      ____ f. scheduling for teachers and students

____ 4. Planning and reflection requirements for teachers

____ 5. In-service and other opportunities for teachers (Standards for Teaching, pp. 37–39)

____ 6. Observation and evaluation of teachers

____ 7. Procedures for selection and review of textbooks and classroom materials

____ 8. Teachers' role in curriculum development and implementation

____ 9. Community's role in curriculum development and implementation

____ 10. Procedures for dealing with controversial issues and/or materials

____ 11. Special education teachers

____ 12. Reading teachers

____ 13. Speech pathologists

____ 14. Gifted program teachers

____ 15. Social adjustment teachers, including drop-out prevention and in-school suspension

____ 16. Dean of boys/girls

____ 17. Music, art, and drama teachers

____ 18. Other special teachers (bilingual, physical education)

____ 19. Procedures for mainstreaming students

Notes:

V.   Person in Charge of Student Discipline

NAME OF PERSON INTERVIEWED: _____

TITLE OF PERSON INTERVIEWED: _____

DATE, TIME, AND PLACE OF INTERVIEW: _____

APPROXIMATE LENGTH OF INTERVIEW: _____

___ 1. School policies/regulations regarding student behavior and appearance

___ 2. Student handbook

___ 3. Procedures for severe discipline referrals

___ 4. Substance-abuse programs

___ 5. Dropout prevention programs

___ 6. School-administered discipline

___ 7. Referrals to other agencies

___ 8. Involvement of law enforcement in the school

Notes:

continued

VI. Principal or Assistant Principal

NAME OF PERSON INTERVIEWED: _____

TITLE OF PERSON INTERVIEWED: _____

DATE, TIME, AND PLACE OF INTERVIEW: _____

APPROXIMATE LENGTH OF INTERVIEW: _____

___ 1. School policies/regulations regarding teacher behavior and appearance

___ 2. Faculty handbook

___ 3. Faculty meetings (time and how used)

___ 4. Organizational pattern of local schools (i.e., board, central office, and/or school)

___ 5. Specialized type of school, such as magnet

___ 6. Specialized programs, such as before- and after-school programs and preschool or childcare programs

___ 7. Information about the community served by the school

___ 8. Community and parent involvement in the school

___ 9. Business involvement in the school

___ 10. Professional organizations (union and/or academic)

___ 11. Teachers' extra responsibilities

___ 12. Student employment opportunities and procedures to follow:

Notes:

FORM 24A

Reflective Observation of Classrooms, Schools, and Curriculum

NAME OF OBSERVER: _____

DATE AND TIME OF OBSERVATION: _____

TEACHER/SCHOOL: _____

GRADE LEVEL AND/OR SUBJECT: _____

OBJECTIVE OF OBSERVATION: _____

_____

Instructions to the Observer: On a separate sheet of paper, respond to the questions below.

1. **Select**
   a. What did you observe about the classroom that was different from and/or similar to your past experience?
   b. What did you observe about the school that was different from and/or similar to your past experience?
   c. What did you observe about the curriculum that was different from and/or similar to your past experience?
   d. What principles did you use from the INTASC Standards?

2. **Describe**
   a. Briefly describe your anecdotal observations of the school.
   b. Briefly describe your structured observation of strategies that challenge students' multiple intelligences.
   c. Did the school have the resources/materials that you expected it to have? Describe.

3. **Analyze**
   a. How has the curriculum changed since you were in elementary/high school?
   b. How did your observation of multicultural/antibias education compare/contrast to your own school experience?

4. **Appraise**
   a. What did you learn from these observations?
   b. How effective were you in completing the forms related to curriculum and technology?
   c. What sources of information about schools, classrooms, and curriculum were most helpful to you?

5. **Transform**
   a. What did you learn about technological resources that can help you in your teaching?
   b. What new knowledge and skills will you incorporate in your teaching?

Source: Adapted from North Carolina State Department of Public Instruction. *Performance Based Licensure*, Raleigh, NC, 1998–1999.

FORM 25A

Anecdotal Record for Observing Students

NAME OF OBSERVER: _____

DATE AND TIME OF OBSERVATION: _____

LENGTH OF OBSERVATION: _____

PERSON AND/OR EVENT OBSERVED: _____

GRADE LEVEL AND/OR SUBJECT: _____

OBJECTIVE OF OBSERVATION: _____

_____

Instructions to the Observer: Write a detailed account of your subject, noting his or her appearance, background, abilities, interaction with others, habits, class responsiveness, behavior, and so on. Try to be as objective as possible.

FORM 26A

Shadowing Form

NAME OF SHADOWED STUDENT: _____

NAME OF OBSERVER: _____

DATE AND TIME OF SHADOW: _____

GRADE LEVEL AND/OR SUBJECT: _____

OBJECTIVE OF SHADOW: _____

GENERAL DESCRIPTION OF LOCATION: _____

Instructions to the Observer: Select a student to shadow for an entire school day. Use a separate page for each class period or segment of the school day you observe. Every five to fifteen minutes, record what the subject of the observation is doing; also indicate what other students and teachers are doing. At the end of the day, summarize the shadowing experience. If possible, interview the student and report the results.

SUBJECT/CLASS: _____

Time (recorded every five to fifteen minutes)	What Subject Was Doing	What Classmates and Teacher Were Doing

continued

SUBJECT/CLASS:

Time	What Subject Was Doing	What Classmates and Teacher Were Doing

The following should be completed at the end of the shadowing experience.

1. **Overview:** Summarize how the student seemed to be involved, how the student interacted with teachers and peers, what the student seemed to learn, and how the student seems to feel about the class.

2. **Report of interview with student:**

FORM 27.1A

Profile Card of Student 1

NAME OF OBSERVER: _____

STUDENT: _____

DATE AND TIME OF OBSERVATION: _____

GRADE LEVEL AND/OR SUBJECT: _____

LOCATION: _____

OBJECTIVE OF OBSERVATION: _____

Instructions to the Observer: Record your observations in five minute intervals.

Time (recorded every five minutes)	Student's Activities/Attitudes

FORM 27.2A

Profile Card of Student 2

NAME OF OBSERVER: _____

STUDENT: _____

DATE AND TIME OF OBSERVATION: _____

GRADE LEVEL AND/OR SUBJECT: _____

LOCATION: _____

OBJECTIVE OF OBSERVATION: _____

Instructions to the Observer: Record your observations in five minute intervals.

Time (recorded every five minutes)	Student's Activities/Attitudes

FORM 28A

Descriptive Profile Chart

PLOTTED BY: _____

DATE AND TIME OF OBSERVATION: _____

STUDENT: _____

SCHOOL: _____

GRADE LEVEL: _____

INTERVAL: _____

OBJECTIVE OF OBSERVATION: _____

Instructions to the Observer: Record brief phrases to indicate the activities of the student during discussion and work periods. Place student activities under "application" if they show involvement in the lesson; if not, place them under "distraction".

| DISCUSSION PERIOD | | WORK PERIOD | |
Application	Distraction	Application	Distraction

Source: Adapted from John Devor. *The Experience of Student Teaching,* 1964.

FORM 29A

Coding System to Observe Student Participation in Lessons

NAME OF OBSERVER: _____

DATE AND TIME OF OBSERVATION: _____

STUDENT: _____

GRADE LEVEL: _____

TOPIC: _____

OBJECTIVE OF OBSERVATION: _____

Instructions to the Observer: Place a slash [/] in the appropriate column to indicate student activities during a single lesson.

Important Contributions	Minor Contributions	Distracting Remarks

FORM 30A

Incomplete Sentence Inventory

OBSERVER'S NAME: _____

DATE AND TIME OF OBSERVATION: _____

STUDENT: _____

GRADE LEVEL AND/OR SUBJECT: _____

OBJECTIVE OF OBSERVATION: _____

Instructions to the Observer: Determine the purpose of completing an informal inventory. Then design some incomplete sentences related to your objective. A sample answer for the first question should be provided in the instructions to the student. Observer can read incomplete sentences to children who are unable to read.

Instructions to the Student: Complete each sentence as honestly and completely as possible. For example, you might complete the first question as follows: When I get home from school I usually play outside.

_____

_____

_____

1. _____

_____

2. _____

_____

3. _____

_____

4. _____

_____

5. _____

_____

6. _____

_____

7. _____

8. _____

_____

9. _____

_____

FORM 31A

Tally Chart of Student-Group Selections

NAME OF OBSERVER: _____

DATE AND TIME OF OBSERVATION: _____

SCHOOL: _____

OBJECTIVE OF OBSERVATION: _____

Instructions to the Observer: List students on left side. Then tally the first, second, and third choices made by each student in the chart below.

Chosen Choosers																									
Chosen 1																									
Chosen 2																									
Chosen 3																									
Totals																									

Source: Frederick J. McDonald. *Educational Psychology,* 2nd ed., Wadsworth Publishing, 1965, 634.

FORM 32A

Sociogram Based on Charted Student Preferences

NAME OF OBSERVER: _____

DATE AND TIME OF OBSERVATION: _____

SCHOOL: _____

GRADE LEVEL AND/OR SUBJECT: _____

OBJECTIVE OF OBSERVATION: _____

Instructions to Observer: Use the tally chart of student group selections to put the names of the most-selected students in a prominent place on the page. Identify males by placing their names in circles, females by placing their names in boxes. Then, put the names of students selected by those few most-selected students next to them. If they selected each other, connect them with a dotted line. If not, draw an arrow to the student selected. Proceed in this fashion until all names are represented on the form.

FORM 33A

Reasonable Public School Expectations for Students

NAME OF OBSERVER: _____

DATE AND TIME OF OBSERVATION: _____

SCHOOL/TEACHER: _____

STUDENT: _____

GRADE LEVEL AND/OR SUBJECT: _____

AREA OF IDENTIFICATION (DISABILITY, IF KNOWN): _____

OBJECTIVE OF OBSERVATION: _____

Instructions to the Observer: What follows is a checklist of reasonable performance and behavior that teachers can expect from nondisabled students. In order to develop an Individual Educational Plan (IEP) for a disabled student, it is necessary to determine which of these expectations he or she is able to meet with no curriculum or classroom modifications. In the right-hand column, indicate the extent to which the student is successful in each of these categories. Note that some of this information may be available only from the student's academic file or teacher; it is important that you make no assumptions and obtain appropriate documentation.

Developmental Areas	Very	Moderate	Limited	None
A. Academic Development				
1. Reading				
2. Writing				
3. Mathematics				
B. Social Development				
1. Interaction with other students				
2. Interaction with teacher or other staff				
C. Physical Development				
1. Uses regular transportation to school; walks or rides school bus				
2. Reports to homeroom or other central location by her/himself				
3. Obeys school rules with other students				
4. Goes to class with regular curriculum				
a. regular volume of curriculum				
b. regular rate of presentation of material				
c. at a reading level that is grade-level appropriate				
5. Has homework assignments in every class				
6. Changes classes when the bell rings				
7. Mingles in hallway before next class				
8. Has lunch with other youngsters				
9. Goes to gym/PE with other youngsters				

Developmental Areas	Very	Moderate	Limited	None
10. Dresses for gym/PE				
11. Goes to the restroom as classes change				
12. Has recess/free time with others				
13. Attends regular school assemblies				
14. Takes regular tests without modifications				
15. Participates in extracurricular activities				
16. Goes on school field trips or outings				
17. Does homework each night				
18. Takes homework back to teacher each day				
19. Attends school each day with very few excused absences				
20. Makes up work if absent				

Source: Adapted from a form used by the Asheville, North Carolina, public schools.

FORM 34A

Information-Processing Categories of Instructional Modifications

NAME OF OBSERVER: _____

DATE AND TIME OF OBSERVATION: _____

SCHOOL/TEACHER: _____

STUDENT: _____

GRADE LEVEL AND/OR SUBJECT: _____

AREA OF IDENTIFICATION (DISABILITY, IF KNOWN): _____

OBJECTIVE OF OBSERVATION: _____

Instructions to the Observer: What follows is a checklist of modifications targeted to the disabled student. Any variety of these modifications may be needed in order for a disabled student to be successful in the school or classroom environment and/or to achieve curricular goals. Observe a disabled student who is in the regular classroom, and check [✓] those modifications that are currently being employed. If a modification is needed but is not currently employed, place an asterisk [*] to the left of the item.

Note: It may be necessary to interview the classroom teacher to determine whether some of these items are currently employed.

Reception Modifications

Vision Reception
___ seating preference
___ auditory/multisensory (earphones, presentations, textbooks, tests, tapes) prompts
___ adjusted evaluation measures, assignments, tests (may have handwriting or spelling errors)
___ computer with voice synthesizer
___ buddy system

Processing Modifications

Processing: Attention
___ teacher prompts
___ preferential seating
___ resource room
___ small-group setting
___ behavior contract
___ multisensory prompts
___ computers
___ taped lecture or teacher notes
___ smaller tasks

Expressive Modifications

Expressive: Oral
___ extra time for responding
___ written answers or sign language
___ buddy system for reports
___ ask questions that students are capable of answering

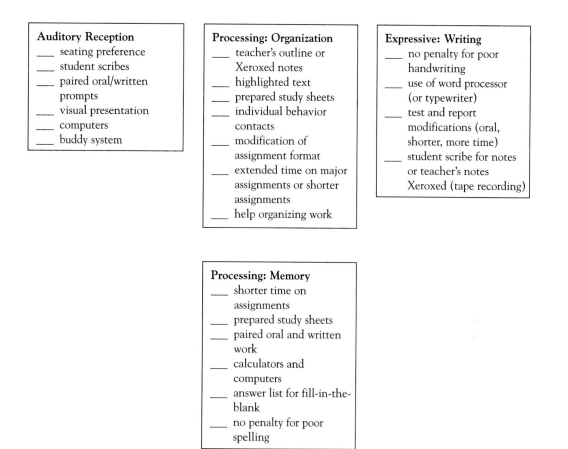

Auditory Reception
___ seating preference
___ student scribes
___ paired oral/written prompts
___ visual presentation
___ computers
___ buddy system

Processing: Organization
___ teacher's outline or Xeroxed notes
___ highlighted text
___ prepared study sheets
___ individual behavior contacts
___ modification of assignment format
___ extended time on major assignments or shorter assignments
___ help organizing work

Expressive: Writing
___ no penalty for poor handwriting
___ use of word processor (or typewriter)
___ test and report modifications (oral, shorter, more time)
___ student scribe for notes or teacher's notes Xeroxed (tape recording)

Processing: Memory
___ shorter time on assignments
___ prepared study sheets
___ paired oral and written work
___ calculators and computers
___ answer list for fill-in-the-blank
___ no penalty for poor spelling

Source: Adapted from a form used by the Asheville, North Carolina, public schools: *Reception Modifications.*

FORM 35A

Reflective Observation of Students

NAME OF OBSERVER: _____

DATE AND TIME OF REFLECTIVE RECORD: _____

TEACHER/SCHOOL: _____

GRADE LEVEL AND/OR SUBJECT: _____

OBJECTIVE OF OBSERVATION: _____

Instructions to the Observer: On a separate sheet of paper, respond to the following questions after you have completed your observation.

1. **Select**
   a. What anecdotal observations of students did you complete?
   b. What structured observation of students did you complete?
   c. What principles from INTASC Standards did you address?

2. **Describe**
   a. What are the unique characteristics that distinguish these students from others you have observed (e.g., needs, background, learning styles, prior experiences)?
   b. What steps did you take to assess the needs of these students?
   c. From whom and in what ways did you solicit information about the students' experiences, learning behaviors, and needs?

3. **Analyze**
   a. How will your assessment of the characteristics and needs of these students affect your planning, tutoring, and teaching?
   b. How did the cultural, ethnic, and racial characteristics of these students influence you and your interactions with them?

4. **Appraise**
   a. What sources of information were most helpful to you as you consider planning and teaching these students?
   b. What observation(s) improved your understanding of the diverse needs of students at this age/grade?

5. **Transform**
   a. What did you learn about the diverse nature and needs of students?
   b. What new knowledge and skills will you incorporate in your teaching?

Source: Adapted from North Carolina State Department of Public Instruction. *Performance Based Licensure*, Raleigh, NC, 1998–1999.

FORM 36A

Anecdotal Record of Preteaching Activities

STUDENT: _____

TEACHER: _____

GRADE LEVEL: _____

DATE: _____

OBJECTIVE: _____

Instructions to Student Participant: Keep an account of the activities you participated in prior to actual teaching. Indicate how you felt about each day's events.

FORM 37A

Checklist of Routines for Helping the Teacher

STUDENT: _____

TEACHER: _____

GRADE LEVEL AND/OR SUBJECT: _____

DATES: _____

OBJECTIVE: _____

Instructions to Student Participant: All of the following duties are important to the management of the instructional environment. You will need to learn to complete these while simultaneously teaching the students and managing the class. To help you learn to do so efficiently, complete all tasks appropriate to your teaching situation and indicate the date each is accomplished. Please have the classroom teacher sign this form when all appropriate activities have been successfully completed.

Activity   **Date Completed**

1. Make a seating chart . . . .
2. Take attendance . . . .
3. Run errands for the classroom teacher . . . .
4. Help with classroom housekeeping . . . .
5. Organize materials needed for a lesson . . . .
6. Make copies of materials needed for the lesson . . . .
7. Help pass out materials to the students . . . .
8. Arrange a bulletin board . . . .
9. Check out books from the library to be used by students in the classroom . . . . .
10. Check out media to be used in a lesson . . . .
11. Make a chart or graph . . . .
12. Make a transparency or stencil . . . .
13. Run a film, filmstrip, videotape, etc. . . . .
14. Get supplementary materials needed for a lesson (magazine illustrations, pamphlets, maps, etc.) . . . .
15. Develop a bibliography for an upcoming unit . . . .
16. Correct papers . . . .
17. Set up or help set up a lab . . . .
18. Write news/assignments on the chalkboard . . . .
19. Set up a learning center . . . .
20. Set up an experiment or a demonstration . . . .
21. Obtain a speaker to come to class, or help organize a class field trip . . . .
22. Help gather materials for a class party . . . .
23. Help make costumes for a class play . . . .
24. Send out a class newsletter to parents . . . .
25. Other (please list below): . . . .

I certify that the student participant listed above has successfully completed all of the above activities that are appropriate to my classroom.

_____

(Classroom teacher's signature)

FORM 38A

Checklist of Routines Involving Students

STUDENT: _____

TEACHER: _____

GRADE LEVEL AND/OR SUBJECT: _____

DATES: _____

OBJECTIVE: _____

Instructions to Student Participant: All of the following activities are important to the instruction of the students. You will need to learn to complete these while simultaneously teaching the students and managing the class. To help you learn to do so efficiently, complete all tasks appropriate to your teaching situation and indicate the date each is accomplished. Please have the classroom teacher sign this form when all appropriate activities have been successfully completed.

Activity	Date Completed

1. Orient a new student . . . .
2. Help individual students with seatwork . . . .
3. Work with a club or student activity . . . .
4. Assist a small group . . . .
5. Work with an individual student in a lab (i.e., computer, language, or science) . .
6. Assist a disabled student . . . .
7. Assist students with library research . . . .
8. Monitor a test . . . .
9. Collect money . . . .
10. Hand out and collect materials . . . .
11. Listen to an individual student read or recite a lesson . . . .
12. Give a test or a quiz . . . .
13. Assist young children with clothing . . . .
14. Bring books or materials to share with the students . . . .
15. Supervise students outside the classroom . . . .
16. Read aloud or tell a story . . . .
17. Help students in a learning center . . . .
18. Accompany students to a school office, the bus, or the playground . . . .
19. Attend a parent-teacher conference . . . .
20. Work with the teacher in developing an IEP (Individual Education Plan) for a mainstreamed student . . . .
21. Accompany students to before- or after-school programs . . . .
22. Help monitor the hallway, lunchroom, or playground . . . .
23. Other (please list below):

I certify that the student participant listed above has successfully completed all of the above activities that are appropriate to my classroom.

_____
(Classroom teacher's signature)

FORM 39A

Lesson Plan Form 1

STUDENT: _____

TEACHER: _____

GRADE LEVEL AND/OR SUBJECT: _____

DATE AND TIME: _____

OBJECTIVE: _____

Instructions to the Student Participant: Whether your plan covers several classroom sessions or only one, each lesson should include an outline of your goal, objectives, materials, and expected lesson duration in addition to the seven steps listed below.

Goal: _____

_____

Objectives: _____

_____

_____

Materials: _____

_____

Duration: _____

_____

FIRST CLASS

1. Anticipatory Set

2. Objective

2

3. Teacher Input

SECOND CLASS

4. Checking for Understanding

5. Guided Practice

6. Independent Practice

7. Closure

FORM 40A

Lesson Plan Form 2

STUDENT: _____

TEACHER: _____

GRADE LEVEL AND/OR SUBJECT: _____

TOPIC: _____

DATE AND TIME: _____

Instructions to the Student Participant: Whether your plan covers several classroom sessions or only one, each lesson should include an outline of your objectives, procedures, materials, and evaluation. Complete the following form.

Objectives: Students will be able to:

Procedures:

Materials:

Website:

Evaluation:

FORM 41A

Unit Plan Format

STUDENT: _____

TEACHER: _____

GRADE LEVEL AND/OR SUBJECT: _____

DATE: _____

UNIT: _____

DURATION: _____

OBJECTIVE: _____

Instructions: Complete items one through six as you plan your unit. Then complete "General Comments."

1. Overview:

2. Purpose:

3. Objectives:

4. Activities:

5. Resources/Materials Needed:

continued

6. **Tying It All Together:**

   Evaluation:

   General Comments:

FORM 42A

Reflective Observation of Preteaching and Planning

NAME OF OBSERVER: _____

DATE AND TIME OF REFLECTIVE OBSERVATION: _____

TEACHER/SCHOOL: _____

GRADE LEVEL AND/OR SUBJECT: _____

OBJECTIVE OF OBSERVATION: _____

Instructions to the Observer: On a separate sheet of paper, respond to the following questions after you have completed participation, preteaching, and planning.

1. **Select**
   a. What preteaching activities did you do?
   b. What kind of planning precedes teaching?
   c. What principle from INTASC Standards did you address?

2. **Describe**
   a. List the steps you used in the planning process.
   b. Describe the parts of your lesson plan.
   c. Describe the parts of your unit plan.

3. **Analyze**
   a. If you have utilized more than one lesson planning format, which was most successful? Why?
   b. How do you relate planning a lesson to teaching a lesson?
   c. How did your preteaching and planning prepare you for your future teaching?
   d. Which preteaching activities were most helpful to you?

4. **Appraise**
   a. What planning techniques were most helpful to you?
   b. How effective were you in checking classroom routines?
   c. How effective were you in checking students' routines?

5. **Transform**
   a. What lesson and/or unit planning techniques will you use in your future teaching? Why?
   b. What additional planning skills would you like to develop?
   c. What did you learn about planning for using the Internet that you can use in your classroom teaching?

Source: Adapted from North Carolina State Department of Public Instruction. *Performance Based Licensure*, Raleigh, NC, 1998–1999.

FORM 43A

Checklist of Tutoring Activities

STUDENT: _____

NAME OF PUPIL(S) TUTORED (IF APPROPRIATE): _____

TEACHER: _____

GRADE LEVEL AND/OR SUBJECT: _____

DATES: _____

OBJECTIVE: _____

Instructions to Student Participant: Listed below and on the following pages are several types of short-term and long-term tutoring activities in which you can participate. As you complete these activities, indicate the date each is accomplished. At the end of each section there is space for your comments about what you learned from the tutoring activities. Please have the classroom teacher sign this form when your activities have been completed.

Short-Term, Informal Tutoring Activities	Date Completed

1. Ask individual students questions about something they are reading or writing, a picture they are drawing, or a project they are working on.

2. Discuss with individual students, stories they have read.

3. Help students with their seatwork.

4. Answer questions students have about their individual work.
   Comment on what you learned from these activities:

Long-Term, Planned Tutoring Activities   Date Completed

1. Teaching skills that have not been mastered by individual students (grammar, composition, reading, mathematical computations, times tables, word problems, word processing, using a computer program, using a table of contents, reading a textbook for meaning, cutting out objects, using a microscope, etc.). List the skill(s) you taught:

2. Diagnosing a student's strength or weakness (administering a specific individual test, listening to a student read, asking a student questions on a variety of levels, watching a student do a mathematical computation, observing a student using a computer program, watching a student use a piece of equipment, etc.). List the method(s) you employed and what you were attempting to diagnose:

3. Remedying a weakness (helping a student learn to cut out a shape with scissors, assisting a student with rules of phonics or grammar, drilling a student on vocabulary, showing a student how to find meaning in a paragraph, demonstrating for a student how to use a piece of equipment safely, etc.). List the method(s) you employed and the weakness you were attempting to remedy:

4. Developing a special talent (teaching the student a technique of drawing, reading a piece of student writing and providing support and suggestions, listening to a student read and discussing what has been read, talking to a student about a historical event, working with a student on a science project, helping a student complete a woodworking project, teaching basic computer programming, taking the student to a museum, etc.). List the method(s) you employed and the talent you were attempting to develop:

continued

Long-Term, Planned Tutoring Activities   Date Completed

5. Other. List specific long-range tutoring activities in which you have
   participated:

   Comment on what you learned from these activities:

I certify that the student participant listed above has successfully completed those tutoring activities
indicated above.

_____

(Classroom teacher's signature)

FORM 44A

Checklist for Planning a Tutorial

STUDENT: _____

NAME OF PUPIL(S) TUTORED: _____

GRADE LEVEL AND/OR SUBJECT: _____

DATES: _____

OBJECTIVE: _____

_____

Instructions to Tutor: As you complete each of the following in your tutoring plans, indicate the date completed.

Planning Activity	Date Completed

1. Discuss the student you will tutor with the classroom teacher.

2. Discuss possible tutoring topics and techniques with the classroom teacher.

3. Carefully plan an initial "getting-to-know-you" session with the student.

4. Diagnose student strengths and weaknesses as necessary.

5. Check INTASC standards and performance-based principles.

6. Check available curriculum guides to determine skills to be taught and their sequence.

7. Set a specific objective for each tutoring session.

8. Develop a plan for each tutoring session (appropriate plan formats can be found in Chapter Five, pp. 33, 34, 35.

9. Develop strategies that utilize your knowledge of multiple intelligences.

10. Consult appropriate resources for teaching techniques and materials.

11. Make sure all necessary materials are available and copied prior to each tutoring session.

12. Monitor the pupil's progress by keeping a log of each day's tutoring.

13. Discuss student's progress with the classroom teacher. Ask for additional suggestions for helping the student.

FORM 45A

Reflections on Tutoring Activities

NAME OF TUTOR: _____

DATE AND TIME OF RECORD: _____

TEACHER/SCHOOL/GRADE: _____

OBJECTIVE OF OBSERVATION: _____

Instructions: On a separate sheet of paper, respond to the questions below after you have completed your tutoring.

1. **Select**
    a. What kind(s) of tutoring activities did you complete?
    b. Why did you decide to do the kind(s) of tutoring you did?
    c. How did the tutoring activities relate to the student(s) age(s)?
    d. What performance-based standard(s) (the ten principles) did you address? (pp. 37, 38, 39)

2. **Describe**
    a. Briefly describe the pupil you tutored (age, gender, background, etc.).
    b. What special needs/interests did you consider when you planned the tutoring activity(ies)?
    c. What resources did you use?
    d. How did you monitor student progress?

3. **Analyze**
    a. How did your preplanning with the classroom teacher help you in planning for your tutoring sessions?
    b. How did the characteristics of the student affect your planning and tutoring?
    c. Did your tutoring plan allow for modification due to unanticipated student input? How?
    d. Why did you select the teaching strategies you incorporated in your lesson?

4. **Appraise**
    a. How different/similar were your objectives for each tutoring session?
    b. How effective were you in using available resources for your tutoring?

5. **Transform**
    a. What did you learn about planning for tutoring?
    b. How did you adjust your teaching as a result of student assessment?

Source: Adapted from North Carolina State Department of Public Instruction. *Performance Based Licensure*, Raleigh, NC, 1998–1999.

FORM 46A

Preplanning Small-Group Checklist

STUDENT: _____

TEACHER: _____

GRADE LEVEL AND/OR SUBJECT AREA:_____

DATES:_____

OBJECTIVE: _____

Instructions to Student Participant: As you complete each of the following in planning for your small group, indicate the date completed.

Preplanning Activity   **Date Completed**

1. Discuss possible types of small-group teaching with the classroom teacher.

2. Discuss the assignment of students to the small group.

3. Discuss the classroom teacher's goal for the small group.

4. Consider the needs, interests, abilities, and intelligences of the students who will participate in the instructional group. Discuss these issues with the classroom teacher.

5. Develop an assessment tool or technique that can measure the progress of several students simultaneously. (e.g., Students complete mathematics problems that begin slightly below their level of achievement and continue beyond their level of achievement. Students answer questions about reading samples that are below their reading level and continue beyond their reading level. Students complete multiple-choice items on a leveled vocabulary list. Students attempt to perform part of a one-act play. Students read parts orally in a short play, etc.).

6. Determine a specific objective for each small-group session.

7. Determine which of the behavior-based principles can be addressed in the small-group lesson.

8. Develop a plan for each small-group session. (Appropriate plan formats can be found in Chapter Five, pp. 33, 34, 35.)

9. Consult appropriate resources for teaching techniques and materials.

10. Make sure all necessary materials are available and copied prior to each small-group session.

11. Monitor the pupils' progress by having them complete individual practice exercises related to each session's objective.

12. Discuss the students' progress with the classroom teacher. Ask for additional suggestions for helping the students.

FORM 47A

Small-Group Teaching Checklist

STUDENT: _____

TEACHER: _____

GRADE LEVEL AND/OR SUBJECT: _____

TOPIC: _____

DATE AND TIME: _____

OBJECTIVE: _____

Instructions to Student Participant: Use this checklist while planning and teaching your small group. To be sure that your lesson includes each of the following, check [✓] each item off as it occurs.

Teaching Activity	Appears in Lesson

1. The students' attention is grabbed.

2. The objective of the lesson is related to the students.

3. Prerequisite knowledge is ascertained through questions and answers, a quiz, completion of an exercise, etc.

4. If appropriate, gaps in needed information are filled in.

5. New information, skills, or materials are presented through explanation, demonstration, discussion, etc.

6. Individual tasks are assigned to each group member.

7. Student performance is elicited and monitored through independent work.

8. Teacher feedback is provided to each student.

9. Student work is related to previous and future learning.

10. Students review what they have learned in the lesson.

11. The objective for the next small-group lesson is determined and communicated to the students.

FORM 48A

Reflections on Small-Group Teaching

NAME OF PRESERVICE TEACHER: _____

DATE AND TIME OF RECORD: _____

TEACHER/SCHOOL/GRADE:_____

OBJECTIVE OF LESSON: _____

_____

Instructions: Respond to the following questions on a separate sheet of paper after you have completed your small-group teaching.

1. **Select**
   a. What were the characteristics (age, gender, background) of the pupils in your small group?
   b. What concepts/skills did you address?
   c. What performance-based standards (the ten principles) did you address (pp. 37, 38, 39)?

2. **Describe**
   a. What diverse student needs did you consider in planning to teach the small groups?
   b. Briefly describe the resources/materials you used.
   c. How did you address multiple intelligences?
   d. What teaching strategies did you incorporate in your lesson?

3. **Analyze**
   a. How did your assessment of prior student learning influence your lesson?
   b. How did the characteristics of the pupils affect your planning and teaching?
   c. What performance modes did you use (e.g., writing, speaking, art)?
   d. How did you modify your plan and teaching to adjust to the unexpected?

4. **Appraise**
   a. How successful was your teaching? What was most effective? What was least effective?
   b. What did the students learn?

5. **Transform**
   a. What did you learn about selecting and using varied teaching strategies?
   b. What did you learn about planning for teaching a small group?

Source: Adapted from North Carolina State Department of Public Instruction. *Performance Based Licensure,* Raleigh, NC, 1998–1999.

FORM 49A

Checklist for Working with Large Groups

STUDENT: _____

TEACHER: _____

GRADE LEVEL AND/OR SUBJECT: _____

DATES: _____

OBJECTIVE: _____

Instructions to Student Participant: As you complete each of these activities, place a check [✔] in the right-hand column.

Activity	Completed

Management of the Classroom

1. Discuss management rules with the classroom teacher.

2. Ascertain consequences for infractions with the classroom teacher.

3. Use only the discipline methods sanctioned by the classroom teacher and the school.

4. Communicate the rules and consequences to the students so that they know you will enforce them.

5. Enforce rules and apply consequences consistently.

6. Do not threaten if you do not intend to carry through on the threat (e.g., "If you aren't quiet, I'll keep you all after school.").

7. Make eye contact with as many students as possible.

8. Call students by name. (Make a temporary seating chart to help you learn names or have the students make, wear, or display name tags.)

Teaching

1. Carefully plan lessons and divide them into clear segments. (Use a planning format such as those in Chapter Five, pp. 33, 34, 35.)

2. Be sure all materials are copied and ready to distribute.

3. Preview all materials prior to using or showing them.

4. Preread anything you intend to use.

5. Maintain instructional momentum (i.e., keep up the pace; do not spend too long on any one element of the plan; do not over explain).

6. Be certain that students understand what is expected (i.e., ask them to explain to you what they are to do; place assignments on the chalkboard prior to the lesson; make sure instructions and printing on handouts are clear; provide clear examples).

Activity	Completed

7. Be sure students know how to perform and are capable of accomplishing the task. (Beware of asking students to do tasks for which they do not have prerequisite knowledge or skills; check with the classroom teacher to be sure they will be able to accomplish what you expect.)

8. Review previous lessons and prerequisite knowledge or skills required for this lesson.

9. Actively involve the students in the lesson.

10. Use teaching methodology appropriate to the subject and the maturity of the students (e.g., labs in science classes, oral reading and independent writing in English and language arts, problem solving in mathematics, research in social studies, etc.).

11. Employ a variety of teaching techniques so that all types of learners can achieve (e.g., audiovisuals, hands-on activities, problem solving, student-designed charts and graphs, laboratories, demonstrations, etc.).

12. Assess students' level of mastery of skills and concepts as often as possible (e.g., classwork that requires demonstration of mastery, observation of students completing classwork, homework that is not merely drill, quizzes, journal entries, writing assignments, etc.).

13. Expect mastery of skills and concepts after a period of teaching, practice, coaching, assessing, reteaching, practice, coaching, etc.

14. Do not expect all students to master all concepts and skills in the same way or at the same time. Group students to provide additional assistance to those who have not mastered important concepts and skills. Use different teaching techniques with these students, or allow those who have mastered the skills or concepts to tutor those who have not.

FORM 50A

Reflections on Large-Group Teaching

TEACHER: _____

DATE AND TIME OF RECORD: _____

GRADE LEVEL AND/OR SUBJECT: _____

OBJECTIVE: _____

_____

Instructions: Use a separate sheet of paper to respond to the questions below.

1. **Select**
   a. What concepts/skills did you address in the lesson?
   b. Why did you address these concepts/skills?
   c. How do these concepts/skills relate to the students' age group?

2. **Describe**
   a. Briefly describe the characteristics of the students (gender, age, race, ability levels).
   b. What resources/materials did you use?
   c. What multiple intelligences did you address?
   d. What role(s) (coach, audience, facilitator) did you play to encourage student learning?
   e. What teaching strategies did you incorporate?
   f. What student assessment technique(s) did you use prior to planning your lesson?
   g. What assessment of students' learning did you apply at the conclusion of your lesson?

3. **Analyze**
   a. How did the characteristics of the students affect your lesson plan?
   b. How did you utilize different performance modes (writing, speaking, reading, doing experiments, solving puzzles)? Why?
   c. Did you modify your plan because of unanticipated events? How?
   d. Why did you select the particular teaching and assessment strategies you incorporated in your lesson?
   e. Evaluate the assessment strategies you used in your lesson.

4. **Appraise**
   a. How successful was your lesson? What was most effective? Least effective?
   b. How did your choice of teaching strategies increase the students' opportunities to engage in critical thinking and problem solving?

5. **Transform**
   a. What did you learn from planning your lesson? What did you learn from teaching the lesson?
   b. What did you learn about the teaching strategies you used?
   c. How did you adjust instruction as a result of the assessment of student learning?

Source: Adapted from North Carolina State Department of Public Instruction. *Performance Based Licensure*, Raleigh, NC, 1998–1999.

FORM 51A

Reflections on Keeping a Portfolio

NAME OF PRESERVICE TEACHER: _____

NAME OF CLASSROOM TEACHER: _____

NAME OF SCHOOL: _____

DATE(S) OF PREPARING THE PORTFOLIO: _____

OBJECTIVE: _____

_____

Instructions: Make a list of the ten performance-based standards, (pp. 37, 38, 39) and refer to them as you respond to the following questions on a separate sheet of paper after you have completed your portfolio.

1. **Select**
   a. What was your objective for preparing a portfolio?
   b. How did you organize your portfolio?

2. **Describe**
   a. List the observation, participation and teaching forms, documents, and artifacts which you selected for inclusion in your portfolio.
   b. Briefly describe assistance you received from classroom teachers, university professors, and peers.
   c. Briefly describe any problems/concerns you experienced.

3. **Analyze**
   a. How did your reflections on completed observations, participation, and teaching help or hinder you as you prepared your portfolio?
   b. How did you decide which forms, documents, or artifacts related to each performance-based standard?

4. **Appraise**
   a. How effective were you in relating your work to the ten performance indicators from the INTASC standards (pp. 37, 38, 39)?
   b. How successful were you in keeping a portfolio?

5. **Transform**
   a. What did you learn about teaching from keeping a portfolio?
   b. What did you learn about yourself as a preservice/future classroom teacher?

Source: Adapted from North Carolina State Department of Public Instruction. *Performance Based Licensure*, Raleigh, NC, 1998–1999.

References

American Association of Colleges for Teacher Education. 1997. *Clinical and Field Experiences: Schools, Colleges and Departments of Education.* Washington, D.C.: Author.

Amidon, E. J., and N. A. Flanders. 1963. *The Role of the Teacher in the Classroom.* Minneapolis: Paul S. Amidon and Associates.

Anderson, L. 1991. *Student Teaching Journal.* University of North Carolina at Asheville. Unpublished manuscript.

Asheville City Board of Education. 1996. *Reception Modification.* Asheville, NC: Author

Association for Childhood Education International. 1977. "Preparation of Elementary Teachers: A Position Paper." *Childhood Education* 73 (3):166,167.

Bliss, T., and J. Mazur. 1997. February. How INTASC Standards Come Alive Through Case Studies. Paper presented at the annual meeting of American Association of Colleges for Teacher Education. Phoenix.

Borich, G. D. 1990. *Observation Skills for Effective Teaching.* Columbus, OH: Merrill.

Boyd, D. 1999. Teaching Styles: Unit 9 Modulers. http://www.aismissstate.edu.ais/ unit9modulers.num. Starkville, MS: Mississippi State University.

Brown, T. J. 1968. *Student Teaching in a Secondary School.* 2nd ed. New York: Harper and Row.

Bruner, J. S. 1960. *The Process of Education.* New York: Vintage

Camp, J. 1997. *Technology Usage in the Classroom or Lab.* Greensboro, NC: University of North Carolina at Greensboro.

Chance, L., V. G. Morris, and S. Rakes. 1996. "Fostering Sensitivity to Diverse Cultures through an Early Field Experience Collaborative." *Journal of Teacher Education* 47, (5) (November, December): 386–389.

Cohen, E. G. 1994. *Designing Groupwork.* 2nd ed. New York: Teachers College Press.

Darling-Hammond, L. 1999. *Reshaping Teaching Policy, Preparation and Practice: Influences of the National Board for Professional Standards.* Washington, D.C.: American Association of Colleges for Teacher Education.

Derman-Sparks, L. 1999. Markers of Multicultural/Antibias Education. *Young Children* 54 (5):43.

Devor, J. 1964. *The Experience of Student Teaching.* New York: Macmillan.

Dewey, J. 1921. *How We Think.* Boston: D.C. Heath.

Duckett, W. R. 1989. *Observation and the Evaluation of Teaching.* Bloomington, IN: Phi Delta Kappa.

Evertson, C. M., and J. L. Green. 1986. "Observation as Inquiry and Method." In *Handbook on Research on Teaching.* 3rd ed., ed. M. C. Whittrock (162–213) New York: Macmillan.

Flanders, N. 1985. *Analyzing Teacher Behavior.* Reading, MA: Addison-Wesley.

Fruend, L. A., and A. Sidney. 1989. "Effective Instruction: Application of the Hunter Instructional Skills Model to Staff Development for Mainstreaming." *ERS Spectrum* 7:28–33.

Funk, S. S., J. L. Hoffman, A. Keithley, and B. E. Long. *Cognitive Behaviors and Verbs.* Tallahassee, FL: Florida State University.

Gagne, R. M., and L. Briggs. 1979. *Principles of Instructional Design.* New York: Holt, Rinehart, and Winston.

Gardner, H. 1993. *Multiple Intelligences: The Theory in Practice.* New York: Basic Books.

Goodlad, J. 1990. *Teachers for Our Nation's Schools.* San Francisco: Jossey-Bass.

Grambs, J., and J. C. Carr. 1979. *Modern Methods in Secondary Education.* New York: Holt, Rinehart, and Winston.

Gredler, M. E. 1999. *Classroom Assessment and Learning.* New York: Longman.

Haberman, M., and L. Post. 1992. "Does Direct Experience Change Education Students' Perceptions of Low-Income Minority Students?" *Mid-western Educational Researcher* 5 (2):29–31.

Hunter, M. 1984. "Knowing, Teaching, and Supervising." In *Using What We Know about Teaching: 1984 Yearbook of Association for Supervision and Curriculum Development.*

———.1985a. "Building Effective Elementary Schools." In *Education on Trial.* E. W. J. Johnson Ed. 53–57 San Francisco: ICS Press.

Jackson, P. W. 1986. *Life in Classrooms.* New York: Holt, Rinehart and Winston.

Joyce, J. 1991. *Student Teaching Journal.* University of North Carolina at Asheville. Unpublished manuscript.

Jones, M., and M. Tadlock. 1999. "Shadowing Middle Schoolers to Understand Them Better." *Middle School Journal* 30 (4):57–61.

Kounin, J. S. 1970. *Discipline and Group Management in Classrooms.* New York: Holt, Rinehart, and Winston.

Lazear, D. 1992. *Teaching For Multiple Intelligences.* (Fastback 42) Bloomington, IN: Phi Delta Kappa Educational Foundation.

Lyons, N. 1999. How Portfolios Can Shape Emerging Practice. *Educational Leadership* 56 (6):63–65.

Manning, M. L. 1993. *Developmentally Appropriate Middle-Level Schools.* Wheaton, MD: Association for Childhood Education International.

McDonald, F. J. 1965. *Educational Psychology.* 2nd ed. Belmont, CA: Wadsworth.

Melton, L., W. Pickett, and G. Sherer. 1999. *Improving K–8 Reading Using Multiple Intelligences.* Bloomington, IN: Phi Delta Kappa Educational Foundation.

Metropolitan Life Insurance Company. 1991. *The Metropolitan Life Survey of the American Teacher: The First Year, New Teachers' Expectations and Ideals.* New York: Author.

Moffett, J. A., and B. J. Wagner. 1992. *Student-Centered Language Arts, K–12.* 4th ed. Portsmouth, NH: Boynton/Cook.

Moore, G., A. Bartlett, and S. Murfitt. 1999. "Preservice Teachers Engaged in Reflective Classroom Research." *Teacher Educator* (Spring): 273–274.

Morehead, M., and D. Cropp. 1994. "Enhancing Pre-Service Observation Experience with Structured Clinical Experiences." *The Teacher Educator* 29 (4):2–8.

Morgan, N., and J. Saxton. 1991. *Teaching, Questioning, and Learning.* New York: Routledge.

Murphy, S. M. 1998. "Reflection in Portfolios and Beyond." *The Clearing House* 72 (1):7–9.

National Assessment of Educational Progress. 1990. *The Nation's Report Card.* Washington, D.C.: U.S. Department of Education.

National Association of State Education Chiefs (NASTEC). 1999. *Field Experiences Required Prior to Student Teaching.* Boston: Author.

National Education Commission on Time and Learning. 1994. *Prisoners of Time.* Washington, D.C.: U.S. Government Printing Office.

National Council for Accreditation of Teacher Education. 1997. *Standards, Procedures, and Policies for the Accreditation of Professional Education Units.* Washington, D.C.: Author.

Nettles, D. H., and P. B. Petrick. 1995. *Portfolio Development for Preservice Teachers.* Bloomington, IN: Phi Delta Kappa Educational Foundation.

North Carolina State Department of Public Instruction. 1998–1999. *Performance Based Licensure.* Raleigh, NC Author.

North Carolina State Department of Public Instruction. 1998. *Social Studies Curriculum.* Raleigh, NC Author.

North Carolina State Department of Public Instruction. 1998. *The Reflective Practitioner.* Raleigh, NC, Author.

Ornstein, A. C. 1990. *Strategies for Effective Teaching.* New York: HarperCollins.

Parsons, T., and E. Shills, eds. 1951. *Toward a General Theory of Action.* Cambridge, MA: Harvard University Press.

Perkins, H. 1969. *Human Development and Education.* Belmont, CA: Wadsworth.

Pierce, D. R. 1996. "Early Field Experiences and Teacher Preparation: Authentic Learning." *The Teacher Educator* 31, (3) (Winter): 217–225.

Pierson, C. A. 1993. "Leadership in Teacher Education." *Childhood Education* 69 (5):288.

Popham, N. 1999. *Comments on Use of a Guidebook for Observation and Participation.* Telephone Conversation. Wilmington College, New Castle, DE.

Sanders, N. M. 1966. *Classroom Questions: What Kinds?* New York: Harper and Row.

Shulman, L. 1994. January. *Portfolios in Historical Perspective.* Paper presented at the Portfolio Conference, Radcliffe College, Cambridge, MA.

Simcoe Board of Education. 1996. *Examination of Curricular Strategies That Challenge Multiple Intelligences.* Midhurst, Ontario, Canada: Author. http://wwwscoe.onca/mm/mmst.num

Sluss, D., and S. Minner. 1999. "The Changing Roles of Early Childhood Educators in Preparing New Teachers." *Childhood Education* 75 (5):280–284.

Sprinthall, L. 1986. An Adapted Madeline Hunter Lesson Plan. In *A Strategy Guide for Teachers: Guidebook for Supervisors of Novice Teachers.* Raleigh: Department of Curriculum and Instruction, College of Education and Psychology, North Carolina State University. Unpublished manuscript.

Sweitzer, A. H., and A. King. 1999. "Student Teachers Explain Changes in Their Thinking." *The Teacher Educator* 34 (1):4.

Ur, P. 1981. *Discussions That Work: Task-Centered Fluency Practice.* Cambridge, U.K.: Cambridge University Press.

U.S. Department of Education. 1998. *Promising Practices: New Ways To Improve Teacher Quality.* Washington, D.C.: Author.

U.S. Department of Education. 1999. *Teacher Quality: A Report on the Preparation and Qualifications of Public School Teachers.* National Center for Education Statistics (NCES). Washington, D.C.

U.S. Department of Education, NCES. 1991. *Trends in Academic Progress* (prepared by NAEP). Washington, D.C.: U.S. Government Printing Office.

Walberg, H., and G. Anderson. 1968. "Classroom Climate and Individual Learning." *Journal of Educational Psychology* 59 (6):414–419.

Wasserman, S. 1999. "Shazam! You're a Teacher." *Phi Delta Kappan* 6 (6):464–467.

Williams, M. J. 1997. *Thematic Social Studies Unit: Government and Economics.* http://ofcn.org/cyber.serv/academy/acc/soc/cecsst/cecsstio.num. Fairbanks, AK Catholic High School.

Wolf, K. 1998. *Self-Assessment: The Reflective Practioner.* Raleigh, NC, North Carolina State Department of Public Instruction.

Yapp, R. H., and B. Young. 1999. "A Model For Beginning Teacher Support and Assessment." *Action in Teacher Education* 21 (1):27–31.

Yinger, R. F. 1999. "The Role of Standards in Teaching and Teacher Education." In *The Education of Teachers.* National Society for the Study of Education (NSSE), Gary Griffin Ed., 85–113 Chicago: University of Chicago Press.